Designed
for
Dignity

Designed
for
Dignity

What God Has Made It Possible
for You to Be

Richard L. Pratt, Jr.

P&R
P U B L I S H I N G
P.O. BOX 817 • PHILLIPSBURG • NEW JERSEY 08865

Library of Congress Cataloging-in-Publication Data

Pratt, Richard L., 1953-
    Designed for dignity : what God has made it possible for you to be / Richard L. Pratt.
        p.   cm.
    Includes index.
    ISBN 0-87552-380-3
    1. Man (Christian theology) 2. Dignity—Religious aspects—Christianity. 3. Self-realization—Religious aspects—Christianity. I. Title.
BT701.2.P69 1993
233—dc20   93-3806

For my daughter,
Becky
May you always live with dignity.

CONTENTS

FOREWORD

I don't know about you, but I grow weary of glib answers to important questions. The existential questions concerning what I'm about, why I'm here, and where I'm going become increasingly important to those of us who have read all the self-help books, taken all the seminars, and listened to all the religious speeches—and who still feel unsatisfied and empty.

It was, then, with a degree of cynicism (albeit a "hopeful cynicism") that I read Dr. Pratt's book on human dignity. I know Richard Pratt, and I know that what he teaches and writes is never shallow and glib. But there have been so many people and so few honest answers to honest questions, that I was careful not to allow expectations to override reality. One learns to be careful in reading books about important issues. Like Christmas, the experience can be ruined if one invests too many hopeful expectations.

If you feel that way, you are in for a very pleasant surprise as you read *Designed for Dignity*. Here is a book—written with great humility, simplicity, and honesty—about people like you and me. But more than that, it is a book about our Creator and the exciting revelation of himself to his people.

Richard has a wonderful gift of taking difficult and abstruse theological concepts and making them understandable and exciting. That is always helpful. However, his book is more than a simplification of difficult ideas. It is a return to the unbelievably refreshing and ever-new truths of the Bible.

Once, upon returning from an extended journey, Thomas Carlyle asked his maid if there was any news. She replied, "Jesus Christ died for sinners."

He replied, "That is old news and new news—and good news."

I commend this book to you. As you read it, you will sense something not dissimilar to the emotion a new Christian has upon first reading the Bible. It is old, it is new—and it is good.

STEVE BROWN
PRESIDENT
KEY LIFE NETWORK

PREFACE

This book is about people—you, me, and the billions of human beings with whom we share this planet. It's a familiar subject to all of us. We live with ourselves and interact with others every day. As much as we are involved with people, we might expect to understand each other better than we do. At least we should have a firm grasp of ourselves as individuals. But try as we may, these mysterious creatures known as *Homo sapiens* still baffle us.

I am not a psychologist, sociologist, or anthropologist, and I am not trying to be one as I write this book. If I am anything, I am a student of theology—more specifically, Old Testament theology. That puts me at a significant disadvantage, because these behavioral sciences offer indispensable insights into humanity. Yet, my interest in the Old Testament also affords me an advantage. The entire Old Testament from Genesis to Malachi—the whole Bible, for that matter—is keenly concerned with what it means to be human.

That may sound a bit odd. We normally think of the Bible as a book about God, not about people. But the Scriptures actually speak of both. In fact, the biblical teachings on God and humanity are so intertwined that we cannot understand one without the other. The more we learn about God, the more we know about ourselves. Similarly, the more we learn about ourselves, the more we know about God. Biblical writers understood this, and so they wrote both about God and the human race.

This subject first intrigued me about five years ago. At that point in my life, I had completed my formal education and faced the stark reality that I could no longer think of my life as something I was preparing to do. I had settled into a job, my family was as large as it was going to be, and I was rapidly moving toward middle age. "This is my life," I finally admitted. But it wasn't entirely a happy thought. "If that's all there is. . . . " So I began to search for a perspective on my life that went beyond the Christian platitudes I knew so well. I yearned for a more satisfying understanding of why I am here on this earth.

As I have spoken to different Christian groups, it has become apparent that many people face this problem. Sometimes it comes in crisis proportions—a divorce, a debilitating illness, the death of a loved one. What is the sense in all of this? Many of us, however, manage to keep the issue safely in the background. But it still slowly eats away at the joys of life. We find ourselves inexplicably dissatisfied, longing for something more. Whatever your situation may be, God wants you to ask hard questions about yourself: What are you? Why do you exist? He calls you to reflect on what it means to be human.

These chapters deal with three basic issues: What did God make us in the beginning? What have we made of ourselves? What has God made it possible for us to be? I cannot think of any questions more important. They are at the center of our hopes and dreams. They shape everything we do.

In short, this book answers that you and I are *designed for dignity*. Every chapter develops some aspect of this theme. Don't expect to find magical potions that will solve all of your problems. The dignity of human existence always remains somewhat mysterious. I certainly have not discovered all the answers, but I have found small tastes of dignity by following the paths I outline in this book. As you read these chapters, I hope you will also find paths along which you can move forward in awareness of yourself, other people around you, and the God who designed you for dignity.

ACKNOWLEDGMENTS

This book is the work of many people. My secretary and friend, Diana Soule, has devoted countless hours to processing the manuscript. Four students—Brad Trenham, John Van Dyke, Jim Campbell-Robertson, and Janie Pillow—offered careful and very helpful editing. My sincere thanks goes to all of you.

1

FINDING A SELF-IMAGE

A few years ago I came across a newspaper article entitled "The Irony of Being Human." The column reported two events that have haunted me to this day.

In the first story, a young woman was sitting alone in her hotel room. She had left her husband and two children to live with another man, but that evening her new partner had deserted her. Everything was lost—her husband, her children, and now her lover. In utter despair, she shoved the barrel of a .38 caliber pistol into her mouth and pulled the trigger. The police found a desperate note left on the nightstand. "Don't cry for me," the wrinkled paper said. "I'm not even human anymore."

Another event occurred that evening in the same hotel. Just a few floors below, advocates of the New Age Movement gathered in the convention center. After several rousing talks, a well-known celebrity led the crowd in a unison chant, "I am God! . . . I am God! . . . I am God!"

"The irony of being human," the article concluded, "is that people in the same time and place can have such contradictory views of themselves."

The columnist was right. These events dramatically illustrate one of the greatest ironies of human existence. We don't know what to think of ourselves. Some of us feel so worthless that we can hardly stand to live another minute.

Others are so full of self-importance that they lift hands in praise of their own divinity. One says, "I am nothing." Another says, "I am God." Which is true? What does it mean to be human?

In this book, we are going to explore what it means to be human. We will begin by looking at ourselves in a mirror. Can we find a true self-image in this confusing world? How should we look at ourselves?

A BALANCED IMAGE

Going to extremes is natural. We do it in nearly every area of life. Either we eat too much or we starve ourselves on a diet. We sit around like couch potatoes, or we strain our backs lifting a heavy load. We let the kids go wild, or we stifle their spirits.

As that newspaper column illustrated, we also go to excess in the ways we look at ourselves. All of us experience good and bad in our lives; we like some things about ourselves and dislike others. But more often than not, we find it hard to keep a balanced self-image. When we concentrate on the negative aspects of our lives, we end up hating ourselves. When we focus on the positive dimensions, we become full of arrogance. Few people take the desperate step of suicide; not many openly worship themselves. But to one degree or another, all of us tend toward pitiful or grandiose self-images. In some instances, we even go in both directions at the same time.

Is it possible to gain a balanced assessment of our lives? Can we have confidence in our value without falling into arrogance? Can we be humble without losing all sense of dignity? We must search for a way of looking at ourselves that avoids extremes. The only way to find a balanced self-image is to turn to the revelation of the One who made us. We must look at ourselves in the mirror of Scripture.

In recent years, advertisers have encouraged shoppers

to "read the label." Their message has gotten through to me. I used to go to the store and simply buy orange juice, but now I read the fine print for additives and preservatives. I used to just look for potato chips, but now I have to see how much fat and sodium each package contains. It's a bother, but labels tell you a lot about what's inside the package.

In the opening chapter of Scripture, God put a label on the human race. If we look carefully at this label, we can learn a lot about ourselves. Moses reported God's first words about humanity in this way: "Let us make man *in our image,* in our likeness, and let them rule over the fish of the sea and the birds of the air, over the livestock, over all the earth, and over all the creatures that move along the ground" (Gen. 1:26, emphasis added). In the very beginning, our Creator gave us a remarkable label. He called us the *image of God.*

Christians frequently refer to people as images of God. We use the terminology as if everyone understood it, but most of us actually have little idea of what it means. We know that our title distinguishes us from other creatures. We guess that it must be something good. But what precisely does it tell us about ourselves?

The label that God gave you and me has many facets, and we will explore them throughout this book. At this point, however, we want to focus on the balanced outlook it offers. It highlights two sides of human existence: our humility and our dignity. We are humble "*images* of God," but we are also dignified "images *of God.*" To have a balanced outlook on the human race, we must understand both sides of the label that God gave to us (see Figure 1).

HUMBLE IMAGES

The word *image* calls attention to our humble status. In the ancient world of the Old Testament, this term often denoted a statue or figurine—a three-dimensional representation of a person or thing. In the light of this widespread usage, we understand what God meant when he called Adam and Eve his image. They were finite, physical representations of their Creator. As astounding as this description may be, we must not miss how it discloses our humility. We are images of God, but that's all we are—images.

God's Label
for
Humanity
"Image of God"

Humility
IMAGE of God

Dignity
Image of *GOD*

Figure 1. Our Balanced Image

In our day, an age-old lie has become popular again. In one way or another, many groups are teaching that human beings are divine. We are extensions of the Creator, having the potential to be gods ourselves. In its own way, secular humanism has lifted humanity to the place of God; Marxism has done much the same thing. Some religious cults express similar views. In recent years, the influx of Eastern religions into the West has made it increasingly popular to speak of the divinity of humanity.

These teachings may surround us, but one thing remains clear. The Bible insists that we are not gods; we are merely *images* of God. We are not equal with our Maker; we do not have a spark of divinity within us. We are nothing more than creatures that reflect our Creator.

Our humility as creatures becomes even more evident

4

when we notice the kind of material God used to make us in his image. Different sorts of images were common in the ancient world. Archaeologists have uncovered spectacular statues of stone and precious metals, but they have also discovered simple images of clay. Were the first humans made out of something common or something special? What kind of images are we? When God formed Adam, he did not use silver or gold, diamonds or rubies. Adam came from ordinary soil: "The LORD God formed the man *from the dust of the ground*" (Gen. 2:7, emphasis added). The first man was not a splendid, diamond-studded image; he was not shaped from precious metals. He was a clay figure.

To grasp the importance of this portrait of humanity, we have to recognize how sharply it contrasted with widely accepted views in the days when Moses wrote Genesis. Moses had been trained in the courts of Egypt to divide the human race into a hierarchy of classes. Commoners served at the bottom of the ladder, and kings ruled from the top. This scheme reflected more than convenient socioeconomic groupings; it stemmed from Egyptian beliefs about the human race. Common people ranked low on the scale because they were little more than clay; the pharaohs stood above all others because they were divine. Some people were humble creatures, and others were anything but humble. Moses opposed these false views as he wrote the Book of Genesis. He declared to Israel that all people descended from images of clay. From the greatest to the least, every person comes from the dust of the ground.

It is hard today to deny that human beings are but dust. Disease and death have turned us into a vapor. We are here today and gone tomorrow. But we must remember that Moses was not writing about sinful, suffering people. At this point in Genesis, Adam was a perfect man, entirely uncorrupted. Nevertheless, even in the absence of sin and death, Adam and Eve were merely clay figures.

If our perfect parents were such humble creatures, how much more are we! Can there be any doubt that we are

5

only finite creatures? As obvious as this truth appears, many people still run from it. They delude themselves with fantasies of grandeur and hide from the biblical portrait of humble humanity any way they can.

When I was in college, a classmate told me about his first day as a student. In the opening lecture of the school year, his instructor explained why he was a teacher. "A liberal arts education is liberating," he said. "I am here to free you from the shackles of superstition, religion, and morality that your parents forced on you. . . . I am here to give you the freedom to make your own way through life, unhindered by your parents and undaunted by God. . . . I will help you become your own god."

These words shocked my friend. He had never heard anyone talk like that. "Be your own god?" he asked me. "I wondered if all my teachers felt that way."

Sadly, that professor's goal is shared by many teachers in higher education. They may not say it explicitly, but countless university teachers see themselves as those who liberate young people from the humiliating dogmas of God and morality. They tell their students not to submit to the decrees of the Creator, but rather to live as their own creators.

We might expect this kind of attitude from university professors, who are notorious for holding radical views. But visit any major business center and you will be surrounded by large numbers of people who act as if they were gods. They may not boldly proclaim their intentions, but many people in the business community believe that no moral restraints apply to them. They lie and cheat as it suits their purposes; they step on their competitors without a second thought. As Gordon Gekko told us in the movie *Wall Street*, "Greed is good!"

We even encounter these perspectives among our friends and families. Racists treat other groups as inferior because they think of themselves as a step above others. Mothers abort their unborn children because babies would interfere with their personal freedom. Children neglect the financial needs of their aging parents to buy a nicer car. "Look out for Number One" is no longer shameful; it's now considered common sense. People all around us exalt themselves above others. Filled with a sense of their own importance, they act as if they were gods.

My family and I have visited Cape Canaveral several times through the years. We enjoy the rocket sites and scientific displays. Whenever we visit the Space Center, one theme comes through loud and clear. "We have come so far," the tour guides keep saying. "We've accomplished so much in space travel. The potential is limitless!"

No doubt, we have come a long way compared to past generations. The power of those rocket engines is astounding; the space shuttle hanger is gigantic. We have to admire the people who put these things together.

Even so, these accomplishments pale in comparison with what we have *not* been able to do. We were so proud when Neil Armstrong walked on the moon and spoke of "one giant leap for mankind." But going to the moon is a stroll around the block compared to traveling to one of the planets. The moon is barely a stone's throw away compared to the chasms of space that divide the galaxies. Advances in space exploration should never convince us of our greatness. As we learn more about the universe, we see how small we are and how little—not how much—we have accomplished.

Actually, the same thing is true in every area of life. We have surpassed our ancestors in many fields, but we have mastered little. We have minuscule knowledge, a pittance of power, and only a whisper of wisdom. Why? Moses explained it long ago in Genesis. Our limitations are severe because we are images made of dust.

It grieves me to admit it, but self-aggrandizement is seen not only outside the church. Even Christians lose sight of how small they are. I visit many different churches, but one problem comes up nearly everywhere I go. Every church has a few members who think they are a cut above the rest. We've heard the jokes about ministers who refuse to retire until there's a vacancy in the Trinity. We've seen wealthy Christians rule the church with their money. Theologians arrogantly insist that everyone must think precisely as they do. Humility hardly comes naturally, even to those who know Christ. We get a few good ideas and conclude that our opinions are always the best. We recognize that God has given us some gifts and soon we consider ourselves indispensable.

We also raise ourselves above others in our homes. Through the years I've seen many Christian families fall apart. Each troubled home has its unique difficulties, but arrogance is a recurring problem. "It's my way or no way!" we shout at each other. Even in Christian homes we deny that we are humble clay.

It is so easy to think we are grand. It is so easy to believe we are above others. But that myth will be shattered on the day we die. Do you think the world will notice when you pass away? Think again. A few people may attend your memorial service, and close loved ones may miss you. But the church will do just fine without you, and society will continue unhindered. We may believe we have the grandeur of gods, but one day that delusion will end for good.

As we search for a genuine self-image, we must begin where God's label begins—with a full recognition of our humble condition. How are you tempted to forget your humble status before God? We all wrestle with this matter. How do you struggle with self-importance at home, at work, and at church? Cast aside this arrogance whenever it arises. It simply does not accord with what you are. We have true understanding of ourselves only when we recognize that we are humble images of clay.

DIGNIFIED IMAGES

Human beings are humble creatures, but look at our label again. We are images, but we are images *of God*

(Gen. 1:27). God did not make Adam and Eve to resemble rocks, trees, or animals. Nothing so common was in his design for us. Instead, God carefully shaped the first man and woman so that they were in *his* likeness. He determined to make us creatures of incomparable dignity.

This side of Moses' account also represented a radical departure from the common beliefs of his day. In those ancient times, only kings could rightly claim to be images of divinity. Commoners and peasants had no such value; they had no importance. It was their destiny to suffer and die for the gratification of kings. These beliefs were behind Israel's terrible suffering in Egypt. What gave Pharaoh the right to subject the Israelites to cruel slavery? How could the Egyptians justify their attempt to destroy the Jews? The answer was very simple for ancient Egyptians. The lowly Israelite shepherds should not have expected honorable treatment. They had no dignity; they did not deserve any respect. Only Pharaoh represented divine authority on earth.

Moses' words in Genesis directly opposed these lies. He boldly claimed that *all* people were royal images of God. Every descendant of Adam and Eve possessed the same honored status. God bestowed great value and dignity not on a few, but on all of the human race.

Moses' portrait of universal human dignity also challenges the way we look at people today. All around us, people deny the honor that God ordained for human beings. Just as the ancient world spurned the vast majority of humanity as so much worthless dirt, modern men and women have also abandoned the human race to ignobility.

As strange as it may seem, university students often encounter excessively low views of humanity from the same professors who encourage them to act like gods. I remember my own biology teacher presenting both extreme views. He scoffed at traditional religion and asserted that we must be masters of our own fate. Yet, as contradictory as it seems, he also insisted that the human race is nothing more than

9

the result of random evolution—ooze out of ooze and back to ooze. People are nothing more than lucky mud.

The results of deprecating the human race are evident everywhere. What value can we attribute to human life if we are just lucky mud? What becomes of morality and human freedom? As this low view of humanity has filtered down to people on the street, the outcome has been devastating. We deprive ourselves of every vestige of worth; every ounce of wholesome honor dissipates. As I once heard it said, "If we have no dignity, let's live it up! If we have no freedom, let's give it up!" Worn down by failure and meaninglessness, teenagers turn to drugs and adults hide inside their liquor bottles. Many even take the last step of suicide.

In the opening chapter of Genesis, Moses affirmed the dignity of all human life for two reasons. First, he wanted the Israelites to reject the views propagated by the Egyptians. Many of Moses' readers had forgotten how terrible life had been in Egypt. But now he reminded them that Egyptian policies of cruel oppression were contrary to reality. God did not bestow nobility on just a few human beings; everyone was his image. The Israelites serving in Egyptian homes, working in the fields, and suffering under the heavy load of Pharaoh's building projects were designed for dignity and should have been treated as such.

Second, Moses taught the Israelites how they should treat other people in the future. He knew how easy it would be for the oppressed to become the oppressors. Once the Israelites settled in their homeland, the temptation to mistreat the weak and vulnerable would be great. This is why the Law of Moses focused so much on protecting widows, orphans, and strangers (for example, Deut. 14:29; 24:19–21). Mistreating others was contrary to the ways of God. No cruel caste system would hold sway among God's people. Servants were to be treated honorably (Ex. 21:2–11). Judges were to show no favoritism to those who were rich and powerful (Ex. 23:6–9; Deut. 1:16–17). Everyone, even the king, was under God's law (Deut. 17:14–20).

All people were to be treated with the honor they deserved as images of the invisible God.

The biblical view of human dignity addresses our modern world in the same two ways. First, it helps us look at ourselves as we ought. We must learn to deal with a world that constantly assails our own sense of honor. We don't face ancient Egyptian propaganda; few modern people believe that dignity rests in royal lineage. We have exchanged those outdated notions for more democratic ideals. But the world hasn't stopped saying that some people are more valuable than others; it has merely adopted different criteria.

Many people know this harsh reality from their teenage years. "I hate high school," one young woman told me. "Everyone makes fun of me because of the kinds of clothes I wear." Teenagers can be cruel. They look for any excuse to ridicule and mistreat others.

Sadly, adults do the same to each other. We determine human worth by a person's income. We measure someone's dignity by his or her possessions. Education, good looks, and a promising career have become the standards by which we determine the value of our fellow human beings.

Moses' record of humanity's creation offers good news to all who do not measure up to these false modern standards. Our value does not rest in external circumstances. God, the Creator of all, has announced that we are his image—royal images possessing divinely ordained dignity. It does not matter what others say; we are valuable because we are God's special creation. Rich or poor, educated or uneducated, attractive or unattractive—you are the likeness of God.

Surprisingly, many Christians have little sense of the honor they bear as God's images. We look in the mirror every day and see someone who disappoints us. We learn to hate our failures, but we end up hating ourselves as well. We want to be humble, but we lose all sense of our importance.

11

Take another look at yourself. God has declared that the person in your mirror is his regal image. You are not perfect—that should be plain enough. But you are still valuable because you are God's image. In God's eyes, you are as important as any king and as valuable as any nobleman who ever walked on this earth. Discard the lies of the world and joyfully acknowledge the dignity God has lavished on you.

Second, Moses' perspective also teaches us how to treat others. Christians are as guilty as the world in showing favoritism. Our church programs exclude certain groups of people. We ridicule the customs of other cultures and sneer at fellow believers who do not live up to our idiosyncrasies. The Bible's radical commitment to the nobility of all people warns us to forsake these ways. All people deserve to be treated as honorable images of God.

I want you to put this book down for a moment. Go find another person and shake his or her hand. Although you will see a flawed, weak human being, say to that person, "Hello, Your Majesty!" Don't say it as a joke. Let the look in your eyes and the tone of your voice convey sincerity. As you do, you may get a sense of what Moses' readers felt when they heard him describe the first man and woman. These former slaves looked at each other and realized with amazement that they were all of the royal lineage of Adam and Eve. They possessed the dignity of being the Creator's images.

How the world would be different if we lived according to this truth! Family tensions would be gone; bigotry would disappear; war would vanish. If we all looked at each other as God designed us, the world would be a radically different place.

Give yourself this test. What happens as you drive down the road and someone pulls out in front of you? What do you say to yourself as you slam on your brakes? "Look at that! There's the noble image of God"? When you are sitting in an airplane and the mother in front of you cannot stop her toddler from screaming, do you think, "Oh, look at that wonderful likeness of God"? Of course not. We can hardly control the angry thoughts racing through our minds. Instead of honoring God's images, we curse them.

When I was in graduate school, I came out of the subway early one morning and turned into Harvard Yard. Blue lights were flashing from several police cars surrounding the statue of John Harvard. As I walked toward the cars, I saw that someone had poured lime green paint all over the statue. I stood there for a moment surveying the damage and overheard one officer talking to the other. "These kids haven't got any respect for the school," he grumbled. "No respect at all."

What was that officer saying? As far as he was concerned, the desecration of John Harvard's statue was an affront to the university itself. An attack on the image was an attack on the school it represented.

In much the same way, you and I must come to grips with the reality that people around us are visible symbols of God in the world. When we dishonor God's image, we dishonor God. When we unjustly attack his likeness, we attack him. The well-known words of James press the point home: "With the tongue we praise our Lord and Father, and with it we curse men, who have been made in God's likeness. Out of the same mouth come praise and cursing. My brothers, this should not be" (James 3:9–10).

Parents dishonor God when they provoke and abuse their children. Children disrespect their Creator when they rebel against their parents. Husbands and wives mistreat God when they mistreat each other.

Moses made it clear to Israel that God gave every human being a title of dignity. How do you deny the honor that belongs to you? In what ways do you treat others with less dignity than they deserve as God's likeness? We must take God's description of the human race to heart. We are clay images—a powerful lesson in humility—but we are also images *of God*—creatures of wondrous value and dignity.

OUR CHANGING IMAGE

On occasion I come across old photographs of myself. Years ago, I did not have a beard, my hair was much longer, and I had fewer silver strands. When I look at those pictures today, I can hardly believe my eyes. I have changed in so many ways.

As we have seen, Moses presents a beautifully balanced portrait of the human race in the first chapter of Genesis. But his picture raises a serious question. If we are the image of God, humble yet dignified, why do we struggle so much with self-degradation and self-exaltation? Why do our lives seem to contradict what God designed us to be in the beginning? The answer to these questions lies in the fact that the image of God has gone through many changes. The course of human history has left indelible marks on every aspect of our existence. To understand who we are today, we must look not simply at our original state but also at the changes that have occurred since then.

In this book, we will look in detail at the historical development of God's image. Each chapter will focus on a particular stage in human history and explore what happened to us at that time. At this point in our study, however, it will help to sketch a brief overview of these developments.

In chapter 2, we will further explore Adam and Eve in the Garden of Eden. God not only gave our first parents a revealing label; he also gave them a wonderful job description. He commanded Adam and Eve to fill the world with other images of God and to rule over the creation as his vice-regents. This twofold task became a distinguishing mark of human dignity throughout history.

Chapter 3 will give attention to the terrible day when humanity fell into sin. Adam and Eve were dissatisfied with the position that God had given them in creation. They violated their relationship with him by rebelling against his command. In response, the Creator placed a curse on our parents that cast the whole human race into futility and death. The royal image of God fell into the severe ignobility that we all experience even today.

As we will see, however, God did not leave his image to rot under this curse forever. He had a plan to redeem us. This plan unfolded slowly through redemptive history, as related in the Bible. At different times, God gave various gifts and responsibilities to his people. Step by step, he made it possible for his images to move further away from the futility of sin and to closer to his original design for humanity. In the remaining chapters, we will trace this history of redemption. We could stop at any point along the way, but we will concentrate on five major periods during which God entered into special relationships with his people.

After the Fall, God richly blessed the whole human race in the days of Noah (chapter 4). Human sin and violence had so corrupted the earth that God radically interrupted history. He destroyed wicked humanity in the Flood, formed a new world order, and commissioned his redeemed images to serve in that new world.

In the days of Abraham, God chose to bless one family, the Jewish race, with a great honor (chapter 5). He revealed the three things all people must have to reach full restoration as his image. God taught Abraham to trust in divine power, to wait patiently, and to persevere in faithfulness.

At the time of Moses, God moved the family of Abraham another step toward full restoration (chapter 6). He formed the people of Israel into an army ready to take the Promised Land. He provided a larger measure of dignity for his redeemed images by giving them his purpose, guidance, and presence.

The time of David also stands out prominently in God's plan of redemption (chapter 7). This was the time when God formed Israel into a magnificent kingdom. David and the people were blessed with countless riches that provided a fuller taste of their dignity as God's restored images.

Finally, we see that God's image is ultimately restored

only through Christ (chapters 8, 9, and 10). Our heavenly Father sent Jesus to be the Savior of all nations. He is "the image of God" (2 Cor. 4:4), and all who trust in him are "conformed to the image of [God's] Son" (Rom. 8:29). Beyond this, when Christ returns in glory, "we shall be like him" (1 John 3:2) and "we will also reign with him" (2 Tim. 2:12). Through the great work of Christ, God's image becomes whole again.

Many changes have come over the human race throughout history. To understand who we are, we must take these developments into account. As we understand what we have done to ourselves, what God has done for us, and what he will do for us, we see with greater clarity what it means to be human.

CONCLUSION

People all around us are confused about who they are. In this confusion, we vacillate between self-degradation and self-importance. Scripture, however, provides a balanced portrait of human beings. We are images of clay, but images designed to reflect our Creator. In this balanced perspective, we live with humility and dignity. The world offers us many false self-images, but Scripture provides us with a self-image worth finding.

ਵੈ   ਵੈ   ਵੈ

REVIEW QUESTIONS

1. What false self-images have modern people endorsed? How do these false images go to extremes?
2. What does it mean to be the *image* of God? How does remembering this part of our title keep us humble?

16

3. What does it mean to be the image *of God?* How does remembering this part of our title give us dignity?
4. How has God's image changed through history? How did we lose our original dignity? What are the five major steps through which God has been redeeming his image?

DISCUSSION EXERCISES

1. Why is this chapter entitled "Finding a Self-Image"?
2. Glance through an issue of a major news magazine. What perspective on the human race does it propound? Does it exalt or denigrate humanity? Explain your response.
3. Make a list of five things in your life that regularly assault your sense of dignity. How can the biblical portrait of your dignity help you overcome these attacks?
4. Make a list of five things in your life that cause you to think too highly of yourself. How can the biblical portrait of your humility help you overcome these temptations?

2

LOOKING AT OUR JOB

I spend a lot of time on airplanes. I remember well a conversation I once had with a businessman sitting next to me. As we talked about his work, he filled the cabin with vulgarities. So many four-letter words poured from his lips that I wondered if he could utter a single sentence without them. After a while, the fellow asked about my line of work.

"I'm a minister," I said matter-of-factly.

You can imagine his reaction. His eyes got big and his face turned bright red as he stammered, "Uh . . . uh . . . I didn't know. . . . Excuse my French. , , . No offense, . . . right?"

I chuckled to myself as he squirmed in his seat, but I wasn't surprised by his response. I've encountered that kind of reaction many times. Once the man knew my job, that told him a lot about me.

You can tell a lot about most people by the kind of work they do. We usually choose jobs that suit our personalities, and our tasks in life always shape us to some extent. Whether we like it or not, our identity is closely associated with our vocation.

In much the same way, we can gain a better understanding of our design as images of God by looking at the job God has given us. To appreciate our identity as God's likeness, we must look closely at what he expects us to do.

OUR TWOFOLD CALLING

Throughout the centuries, theologians have differed over how humanity is set apart as God's image. What features separate us from other creatures? Some theologians have emphasized our rational and linguistic capacities. Others have pointed to the immortality of the human soul as our most important characteristic. Many theologians have insisted that our moral and religious character distinguishes us from other creatures.

All of these views represent important facets of the truth. Our rationality, immortality, morality, and many other qualities reflect God in the world. In the broadest sense, Adam and Eve were like God in every way possible for finite creatures to be like him. They were limited by time and space, but their minds, wills, and emotions were patterned after their Creator. Even their physical characteristics and abilities reflected the spiritual characteristics and powers of God.

As important as these perspectives may be, Moses explained the image of God by emphasizing the job God gave us to perform in this world. Immediately after making the man and the woman, God gave them a special commission. We read in Genesis 1:28, "God blessed them and said to them, 'Be fruitful and increase in number; fill the earth and subdue it. Rule over the fish of the sea and the birds of the air and over every living creature that moves on the ground.'" This verse commands us to be fruitful, increase, fill, subdue, and rule. These five commands reveal our most basic human responsibilities.

We often call these tasks for humanity the *cultural mandate.* It was God's design that people build an earthly culture for his glory. This cultural mandate involves two basic responsibilities: multiplication and dominion. First, God gave Adam and Eve a commission to multiply: "Be fruitful . . . increase . . . fill." Their job was to produce enough images of God to cover the earth. Second, God ordered them to exercise dominion over the earth: "Fill . . . subdue . . . rule." Adam and Eve were to exercise authority over creation, managing its vast resources on God's behalf. Needless to say, these two mandates cannot be entirely separated from each other. Multiplication involves dominion, and successful dominion requires multiplication. Nonetheless, from the beginning these two sides of the cultural mandate were to be our main tasks in life.

At first, it may seem strange to think of our purpose on earth in terms of multiplication and dominion. Modern people do not normally look at themselves as multipliers and rulers. Yet, upon reflection, ordinary experience confirms what we find in Scripture. God has written this twofold calling on our hearts. He has embedded the ideals of multiplication and dominion deep within the human psyche.

Consider, for instance, how most of us evaluate human governments. History testifies to aberrations, but most people applaud national policies that benefit future generations. Responsible people loathe shortsighted leaders. Why? Because God's call to multiplication is written within us. We were made to care about our progeny. As hard as we try, we cannot fully escape our commission to be fruitful.

Exercising dominion over the world is also part of the human conscience. We approve of political leaders who provide security and prosperity for their citizens. We do not consciously accept faltering economic programs or mismanagement of natural resources. Why do so many people share these ideals? Because we know our commission as God's image.

Our families also take shape around this twofold calling. Most people realize that good parents concern themselves with their children's welfare. Child neglect offends even those who hold to few other moral values. We are all concerned with multiplication. In a similar way, good parents work hard to equip their children for life's tasks. We send them to school and we encourage them to study. Why? We do not want our offspring to miss life's opportunities for dominion.

We may not be accustomed to describing ourselves as Moses did, but common human experiences make it plain that God's call to Adam and Eve is not foreign after all. To deny our twofold commission is to deny our humanity.

What do multiplication and dominion have to do with the image of God? Why did Moses focus on these tasks as he described the human race? To find out, we must journey back to the time when Moses lived—to the days of pharaohs and emperors, pyramids and ziggurats.

Many kingdoms in the ancient Near East stretched across thousands of square miles. The kings of these empires were powerful leaders, but the size of their domains presented serious political problems. How could kings exercise control over their empires? How could they keep order? Ancient kings simply could not maintain personal contact with all regions of their nations. They needed other ways to establish their authority.

Many rulers solved this problem by erecting images of themselves at key sites throughout their kingdoms. They produced numerous statues of themselves and endowed their images with representative authority. Modern museums house the remains of some of these statues. As we gaze upon these imposing figures, their ancient purpose becomes evident. When citizens saw the images of their emperor, they understood to whom they owed their allegiance. They knew for certain who ruled the land.

Moses described the twofold job of humanity against this historical background. To be sure, God did not need to make images of himself; he had no problem filling the earth with his presence. But he chose to establish his authority on earth in ways that human beings could understand. Just as ancient emperors filled their kingdoms with statues of themselves, so God commanded his images to populate the earth. "Multiply yourselves," God said. "I want my images spread to the ends of the world." Just as emperors conferred authority on their images, so God commanded his likeness to reign over the earth. "Subdue and rule," God commanded. "I give you the authority to represent me in my world."

I never understood the power of images until my wife and I visited Eastern Europe nearly a decade ago. As we entered a prominent city in Poland, a colorful sight caught our attention. Brilliant red flags encircled a large open court. Among the streaming colors were several statues of armed soldiers, each standing at least eight feet tall. When I asked our cab driver about the sight, he responded with a heavy accent, "Iz Roosha. . . . Iz Roosha." After a moment, I understood. The statues were figures of Russian soldiers.

A few days later, I shared this experience with a Polish friend. He told me that statues like these stood throughout his country. "They're in nearly every town," he explained, "in the parks and on the street corners." Then with a note of despair he added, "They remind us of who is *really* in charge." Those images of Russian soldiers were not empty symbols; they represented powerful political realities.

In recent years we have seen many news reports from countries that once suffered under the rule of communism. The changes have been remarkable. But the news reports that have meant the most to me have been those showing people tearing down statues of Stalin and Lenin. In one town after another, huge images of the former dictators have come crashing to the ground.

Why did those people waste so much time tearing down statues? Weren't there more important things to do? We have a hard time understanding why so much attention is given to these matters. But if you had lived your life under the shadows of those imposing images, you would grasp why they stand no more. They were powerful symbols of cruel oppression.

Now we can see the importance of our calling as God's

likeness. If inanimate images of finite political figures can be so significant, how much more importance do you and I have as living, breathing images of the eternal God? Look at the honor God has given you and me. He granted us the privilege of proclaiming in all we do that our God is in charge of the world. By filling and ruling over the world, we fulfill our true purpose in life. We reach heights of dignity because we represent the authority of the King of the universe.

Up to this point, we have described our task as the image of God in very general terms. Now we must go further. How are we to multiply and have dominion? What kinds of activity does our twofold cultural mandate entail? We cannot fully explore these complex issues, but we will sketch some of the important contours of both sides of our commission from God (see Figure 2).

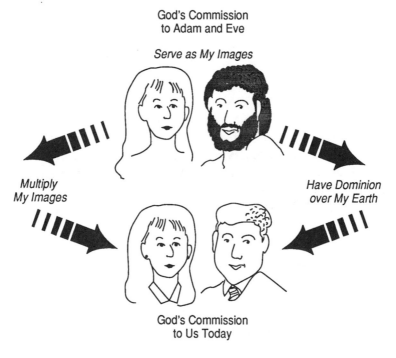

God's Commission
to Adam and Eve

Serve as My Images

*Multiply
My Images*

*Have Dominion
over My Earth*

God's Commission
to Us Today

Figure 2. Our Twofold Calling

MULTIPLICATION

Have you ever noticed how road signs communicate much more than the words they bear? "Sharp Curve" is more than information about the road's direction. It tells drivers, "Slow down and take care." "Deer Crossing" is more than a statement of fact. It means, "Watch out for deer." To understand road signs, you have to acquire a basic understanding of the words, but you also have to remember that they convey more than meets the eye. In much the same way, we must grasp the basic meaning of "Be fruitful and increase in number; fill the earth" (Gen. 1:28) and then explore the vast array of responsibilities implied by these words.

Let's begin unpacking our commission at its most basic level. Simply put, God placed Adam and Eve in the world to have children. To fulfill their God-ordained purpose, our first parents were to reproduce.

This basic meaning of God's command needs to be emphasized today as never before. In many circles, children are looked upon as nothing more than nuisances. They make noise, constantly ask questions, get sick, and cost lots of money. I don't know how many times I have heard young couples say, "We don't want the responsibility of kids. They only get in the way."

If this has been your attitude toward children, you need to ask yourself a question. Just how would children get in your way? Yes, they limit our insatiable pursuit of luxuries and pleasures. They get in the way of careers, expensive cars, and extravagant vacations. But children do not hinder us from becoming what God wants us to be. He designed us to have children.

We have to be careful not to go to extremes here. Bearing children is an important dimension of human responsibility, but we have many other duties that also require our attention. Just as we do not evangelize or help the poor every moment of our lives, God does not expect us to have as many babies as we possibly can. We must balance our call to physical multiplication with our other responsibilities. The age and health of the couple, the constraints of extraordinary vocations, responsibilities for aging parents, financial considerations, and many other factors help us determine the timing and number of our children. Balancing the responsibility of bearing children against all of our other duties requires wisdom. There is a time to multiply and a time to refrain from multiplying (Eccl. 3:1–8). Each couple must determine how God would have them serve him in this way.

Nevertheless, the Scriptures make it clear that physical multiplication is our honorable calling. In a day when children are viewed so negatively, we must strongly affirm the Bible's outlook. The Scriptures speak of sons and daughters as gifts and rewards (Ps. 127:3); they are blessings from God (Ps. 127:5). Children are not a curse. Instead, they are central to God's reason for putting us on this planet. We should encourage each other to multiply and should rejoice with those who bear children.

With the basic idea of multiplication in mind, we may now look further at this command. There is much more to multiplication than mere biological reproduction. Animals were commanded to reproduce (Gen. 1:22), but something much more significant is expected of humanity. Adam and Eve were not just to multiply—they were to multiply *images of God.* God commanded them to fill the world with people who would serve as his regal representatives.

Had evil not come into the world, this job would have been relatively easy. Children would have grown up serving God naturally. With the advent of sin, however, children are not born with a natural propensity to follow the commands of their Maker. Parents have to show them the way. Now multiplication is both a physical and a spiritual task. It involves bearing children, but it also entails training and teaching them to live as images of God.

I remember once visiting a woman who had just given birth to her first child. It had been a difficult delivery, but the mother and daughter were fine. As I started to leave,

26

the woman smiled and said, "Well, I guess I've done my part in filling the earth." But I responded, "No, you've only begun. Now you have to teach your daughter to live like what she is." Multiplication in a fallen world has a crucial spiritual dimension. We fulfill our calling only as we raise our children to serve their Creator.

This spiritual dimension of multiplication helps us understand the special covenant relationship that exists between God and the children of believers. Throughout Scripture, God treats the offspring of believers as those who are expected to be the heirs of saving grace. For instance, the covenant with Noah involved Noah and his family (Gen. 7:1; 9:1, 9). Promises were made to Abraham and his descendants (Gen. 17:7). Moses declared that God's revelation belonged "to us and to our children" (Deut. 29:29). The promises made to David were for him and his descendants (2 Sam. 7:12–16). Even the New Testament affirms that the promise of the Spirit "is for you and your children" (Acts 2:39). The apostle Paul declared that the children of believers are "holy," set apart from the world (1 Cor. 7:14).

The bond established between God and our children does not guarantee their salvation, but we can have a special measure of hope for them. Covenant children are taught the Word of God. They live among the people of God and taste the blessings granted in Christ. They must lay hold of Christ for themselves, but the sons and daughters of believers are expected to be heirs of the grace that is offered through the Savior.

The importance of parenting as an aspect of multiplication stands out in the well-known words of Deuteronomy 6:4–9. Throughout the centuries, Jews have repeated verse 4 as a summary of their faith: "Hear, O Israel: The LORD our God, the LORD is one."

Followers of Christ know the fifth verse of this passage as the greatest commandment in the Bible (see Matt. 22:37–38): "Love the LORD your God with all your heart and with all your soul and with all your strength."

27

But notice the instructions that follow these famous passages: "These commandments that I give you today are to be upon your hearts. Impress them on your children. Talk about them when you sit at home and when you walk along the road, when you lie down and when you get up. Tie them as symbols on your hands and bind them on your foreheads. Write them on the doorframes of your houses and on your gates" (vv. 6–9).

These verses point in two directions. On the one hand, adults are to put the commands of God in their own hearts (Deut. 6:6). On the other hand, they are to teach God's Word to their children (Deut. 6:7–9). God commanded parents to instruct their offspring in his Word at home, along the road, in the morning, and at night.

Why does the mandate to train children follow on the heels of the greatest commandment in the Bible? Why is it given such prominence in the Mosaic Law? The answer is simple. Passing our spiritual inheritance on to future generations is at the heart of our job as God's images. Without spiritual multiplication we fail to fulfill our basic purpose on earth. Through our example, discipline, teaching, and prayers, we lead our children to live as the likeness of God. They in turn pass their inheritance in Christ on to the next generation. Multiplication as the image of God entails all of these spiritual processes.

The task of multiplication is even broader than this. Many times the New Testament employs the metaphor of multiplication when referring to evangelism and discipleship. When Jesus commissioned his disciples to multiply, he said, "All authority in heaven and on earth has been given to me. Therefore go and make disciples of all nations, baptizing them in the name of the Father and of the Son and of the Holy Spirit, and teaching them to obey everything I have commanded you. And surely I am with you always, to the very end of the age" (Matt. 28:18–20).

God adopts all who believe in Christ into the family of the faithful. Through the sanctifying work of the Spirit, he conforms them to the image of Christ (Rom. 8:29). In this sense, we fill the earth with God's images as we spread the message of Christ throughout the world. We fulfill the cultural mandate by completing the gospel mandate.

I have encountered a terrible misconception in some circles. Many single people and couples come to believe that they are second-class Christians because they cannot have children. They think they must marry and have their own natural offspring to be fully human. We must remember, however, that Paul insisted that in some cases "it is good for a man not to marry" (1 Cor. 7:1, 8). The gift of celibacy for the sake of the kingdom is a high calling (Matt. 19:10–12). Moreover, we must not forget that Jesus, the perfect human being, was never married and had no children. He fulfilled his role as a multiplier by calling men and women into the family of God through the gospel.

This is good news for those who cannot have children to raise in the ways of Christ. You are not prevented from fulfilling your call to multiply, because you still have every opportunity to become a spiritual parent. Are you disappointed at the thought of never having a son or daughter? Do you suffer the agony of being childless? Do not despair. Just as Paul called Timothy "my true son" (1 Tim. 1:2), so you can reach out to others with the gospel of Christ and become spiritual mothers and fathers to many children.

Multiplying images of God is a great honor, but it can be difficult to keep a positive attitude. On a day-to-day basis, multiplication is just plain hard work. Do you spend every day chasing little ones around the house? Do you sit in a car most of your time, chauffeuring teenagers from place to place? Do you devote hour after hour to helping your children with school lessons? It doesn't seem very dignified at times. Nobody appreciates you; nobody thanks you; nobody honors you.

Have you given yourself for years to the task of evangelism? You speak to your neighbors, visit the local prison, and contribute hard-earned money to missionaries. What do you have to show for it? A door slammed in your face? A neighbor who thinks you're a fanatic? Where's the dignity in that?

Imagine you are the servant of a powerful medieval king. He summons you to his lavish throne room, where he sits holding his most precious diamonds. You admire their beauty as they sparkle in his hand. But to your surprise the king extends his hand to you and says, "Care for these jewels. Make them bright and shining, so that all may see my glory." How would you feel? What would you think? Every servant would be delighted to have such an important job. How honored you would feel to be chosen for such a noble task.

You don't have to imagine such a world—you actually live in it! The King of the universe has summoned you. He has given you a special task. "Take my precious images," he says to you. "Keep them, mold them, and make them beautiful, so that all may see my glory."

When you raise your children, you are not just reproducing—dogs and cats do that. You are shaping images of the Creator. When you teach someone about Christ, you are not simply spreading a religious ideology. God has entrusted his likeness into your hands. Multiplication is a job you can be proud to do.

Where do you see multiplication occurring in your life? How do you fill the world with God's images? In one way or another, multiplying likenesses of God is a glorious responsibility that should be central in everyone's life.

DOMINION

When heads of state draft soldiers and send them to distant lands, they have some purpose for their actions. Some strategy or goal lies behind their deployment of troops. In much the same way, God deployed his image for a reason. The command to multiply had a goal. Humanity was to do something as it spread throughout the world.

As we have seen, God commissioned the human race to rule over the earth (Gen. 1:28). Multiplication was intended to give God's servants worldwide dominion. But what precisely does this aspect of our divine commission mean? What is dominion over the earth?

In my early years as a Christian, I was attracted to all kinds of radical causes. Once I met a group of believers who had left city life to move out on a farm. They grew their own food and lived as close to the land as they could. I remember asking the leader of the group why they had chosen this lifestyle. His answer came from the Book of Genesis: "God told us to subdue *the earth*," he said. "And that's what we're going to do."

This fellow was right in some ways, but wrong in others. The command to have dominion over the earth was much broader than he imagined. To rule as God's image does not mean that we must all return to farming. It means that we must manage whatever facets of creation God places before us.

The Bible makes it plain that dominion involves many different tasks. In the beginning Adam and Eve were gardeners in Eden (Gen. 2:8), but this limited responsibility was not the full extent of God's calling. God had designed them for ever-expanding responsibilities. In primitive societies people exercised dominion by cultivating the earth and domesticating animals. In the days of David and Solomon, Israel developed extensive communication systems and international trade. Daniel subdued the earth by learning the wisdom of the Babylonians (Dan. 1:4) and ruling as an effective politician (Dan. 1:20; 2:48). Throughout the Bible, our spiritual ancestors exercised dominion in countless ways wherever they went.

Most of us today have little contact with the earth itself. We live in high-rise apartments above cities covered with concrete, or we own a small plot of land surrounding

31

a suburban home. The closest we come to nature is a leisurely stroll through the park or a weekend camping trip. Our lives are largely insulated from the nitty-gritty of the earth. But this separation does not keep us from exercising dominion. We may not hunt for food or clear fields for planting, but we are nonetheless subduing the earth every time we advance any legitimate aspect of human culture. We serve our calling as farmers, bankers, housewives, doctors, artists, secretaries, teachers, and factory workers—the list goes on and on. Our gifts and callings vary, but all of our specific jobs fit within the general mandate to rule over the earth.

This aspect of our God-ordained purpose offers a perspective on work that we need to reaffirm today. We live in a time when people misunderstand the basic nature of work. Many people treat work like a curse. "I hate what I do," they say. "I wish I could win the lottery and just enjoy life." But the biblical outlook is just the opposite. God commissioned Adam and Eve to work before sin and hardship came into the world. The job of exercising dominion was a privilege, not a curse.

Perhaps you feel chained to a kitchen counter. You wash the same dishes time and again. You clean the same house day after day. Maybe you spend your days outside the home, bound to a desk or a workstation. Work is a taxing chore. Your only hope is reaching retirement age. If these are your feelings, something has to change. We learn from Scripture that work is an honor that God gives to his noble images. It is not to be despised, but cherished.

The great King has summoned each of us into his throne room. This time, however, he is not entrusting jewels to us; rather, he is distributing property. "Take this portion of my kingdom," he says. "I am making you my steward over your office, your workbench, your kitchen stove. Put your heart into mastering this part of my world. Get it in order; unearth its treasures; do all you can with it. Then everyone will see what a glorious King I am."

That's why we get up every morning and go to work. We don't labor simply to survive—insects do that. Our work is an honor, a privileged commission from our great King. God has given each of us a portion of his kingdom to explore and to develop to its fullness. This is why Paul exhorted the Colossians, "Whatever you do, work at it with all your heart, as working for the Lord, not for men, since you know that you will receive an inheritance from the Lord as a reward" (Col. 3:23–24). Paul's words speak plainly to us when we grow tired of work. We are to work "with all [our] heart," because we are "working for the Lord."

Indeed, work is not only a privilege but a solemn service we offer to God. Many people love their work because of the benefits *they* derive from it. We devote ourselves to our jobs, but we often do so for the wrong reasons. Materialism motivates us—we've got to have more things. Status motivates us—we all want to be on top. As a bumper sticker puts it, "Life's just a game and the one who dies with the most toys wins."

But God did not call us to have dominion over the earth for our own glory and honor. God *commanded* Adam and Eve; he *commissioned* the human race. We work hard at our tasks so that *God* might be honored.

Military recruiters know how much we are tempted to live for ourselves. They design their slogans to appeal to our selfish motivations: "See the world." "Be all that you can be." "Be one of the few, the proud." I'm sure many recruits are shocked when they step off the bus for basic training. Once they arrive, the sergeants don't discuss travel and self-fulfillment. They insist on sacrificial devotion and service. Why? Because self-centered soldiers don't make good soldiers.

Self-centered images don't make good images, either. Ruling over the earth as God's likeness is a service that often entails forfeiting personal pleasures and gratifications for the glory of God. As Jesus put it, "In the same way, let

33

your light shine before men, that they may see your good deeds and praise your Father in heaven" (Matt. 5:16).

Imagine how different the church would be if Christians recognized that work must be done for God's honor. How many times have the seeds of discord been sown because people do not receive the praise they think they deserve? We work hard in Sunday school; we serve faithfully as officers. We give of our time and energy, but we receive no cards, no phone calls, no applause. Resentment begins to grow and we say to ourselves, "They don't appreciate anything I do. I'll never do another thing for that church." When these attitudes arise within us, we must back away and examine our motives. Why do we serve in the church? What is our purpose—to promote our own honor or the honor of God?

Work outside the church is also a service to God. No work is secular. We should honor Christ in the workplace as much as we do in the place of prayer. We may not pursue any job we desire; we may not work any way we want. We work only as God has commanded. To be the image of God is to receive a calling that requires humble devotion to the glory of God. We are creatures designed to bring honor to the King through our dominion over the earth.

How are you exercising dominion over the earth? How should you consider your work a privilege? How should you change so that you exercise dominion for God's glory alone? We will be able to fulfill our call to subdue and rule over the earth only as we are able to answer these questions.

CONCLUSION

In this chapter we have seen how God gave his image a twofold job. He calls us to multiply and to have dominion over the earth. As we look at our lives in the light of this commission, we discover what we are to do as images of God. We must devote ourselves to the privilege of filling the earth and ruling over it for the honor of God. This is why we were put on the earth. What greater task could be ours?

≀⚊   ≀⚊   ≀⚊

REVIEW QUESTIONS

1. What different aspects of God's image have been emphasized by various theologians? What did Moses emphasize about God's image in the opening chapter of Genesis?
2. How is the cultural mandate appropriate for the image of God? What ancient historical background explains our job as God's image?
3. Explain our commission to multiply. How has sin expanded the spiritual side of this calling?
4. Explain our commission to have dominion. In what two ways should this responsibility affect our view of work?

DISCUSSION EXERCISES

1. Why is this chapter entitled "Looking at Our Job"?
2. Make a list of ten things that you do during a typical workday. Do you associate them with multiplication, dominion, or both? Why?
3. What is the most difficult obstacle you face in multiplication? Why does it hinder you so much? How does the biblical outlook on multiplication help you in this struggle?
4. What is the greatest problem you encounter in exercising dominion? Why is it so difficult for you? How does the biblical outlook on dominion help you in this struggle?

3

SINKING INTO RUIN

When my wife and I bought our first house, the builder offered us a handful of photographs. "Take these pictures with you," he urged. "They'll show you a lot about the house." As we flipped through the snapshots, we noticed that most of them had been taken during the early stages of construction: grading the earth, spreading a bed of special sand, placing steel reinforcement bars, and pouring the concrete slab. We couldn't understand why the builder was so interested in showing his work on the foundation. We were much more interested in things visitors would see: the color of wallpaper, the style of carpet, the kinds of shutters outside. "Why so many pictures of the foundation?" we wondered.

A few months later we found out why. Beneath the topsoil in that region of the country is a slow-moving ocean of mud known as "Yazoo clay." The swelling and shrinking of this clay causes the ground to rise and fall over time. As a result, almost every house built on this clay goes through a process of settling. As one person told me, "There are only two kinds of houses here: those that *have sunk* and those that *are sinking*." "It doesn't matter how nice your house is," he continued. "When the ground gives way, even the governor's mansion will sink."

In the opening chapters of this book, we saw that God

originally created Adam and Eve as his noble images. They were more magnificent than any governor's mansion. But God's original design for human dignity did not last long. The ground began to give way beneath Adam and Eve and the human race sank into ruin.

DECEPTION BEFORE RUIN

How did humanity fall into ruin? What process led to the corruption of our original dignity? Most people are familiar with the story of humanity's fall into sin. God warned Adam and Eve not to eat the forbidden fruit, and they ate it anyway. But the events preceding this act of disobedience are more complicated than we often remember. Adam and Eve did not boldly plunge themselves into the jaws of death. Rather, their decision to rebel against God was preceded by a subtle process of deception.

The Genesis account tells us that Eve encountered Satan in the form of a talking serpent. He "was more crafty than any of the wild animals the LORD God had made" (Gen. 3:1), and he coaxed Eve toward her doom. How did he do this? What was his strategy? Satan's strategy in the Garden of Eden focused on one thing—*human pride.*

The word *pride* always makes me remember an incident that took place after my daughter's first-grade play. After the performance, the teacher congratulated the class. "You should be proud of yourselves, boys and girls," she said. "You did a great job!"

That afternoon my daughter came home terribly frustrated. She burst into my study and shouted, "My teacher did a bad thing today!"

"What's that?" I asked.

"She said we should be proud, but you and Mommy said to be proud is bad!"

My daughter was right. We had taught her that "pride goeth before destruction, and an haughty spirit before a fall" (Prov. 16:18, KJV). She knew that pride was the source of many evils in the world.

On that day, however, we had to explain that the word *pride* has more than one meaning. Sometimes it has positive connotations. "Have some pride," we say. "Don't be ashamed of who you are." We want our children to have this kind of legitimate self-esteem, and we tell them to delight in their religious heritage, nation, and family. We all need a measure of such positive pride.

But other times we speak of pride in a negative sense, as an attitude that people should avoid. "Don't be so proud of yourself," we caution. "People will think you are the most arrogant person in the world." This kind of pride amounts to nothing more than wicked self-conceit. We teach our children to avoid it; we try to keep ourselves from it as well.

Most of the time, Christians assume that Adam and Eve fell into sin only because they thought too highly of themselves. "Their arrogance led them to rebel," we say. This view is true as far as it goes. But as we will see, Adam and Eve had difficulties with both kinds of pride. Satan first robbed them of legitimate pride and then led them to defy their Maker.

The first step in Satan's deception becomes clear when we recognize the honor that God had bestowed on Adam and Eve. Our first parents should have looked on themselves with a high level of self-respect because God treasured them so much. Several aspects of Moses' account reveal the special status Adam and Eve had been given in God's creation.

First, Adam and Eve should have taken positive pride in their tremendous opportunity. God had placed them in Eden to serve as his gardeners. He had commissioned Adam "to work [the garden] and take care of it" (Gen. 2:15).

In modern times we do not think of gardening as a very high calling, but Eden was no ordinary garden. It was "the garden of God" (Ezek. 31:9), the palace garden of the great King. Adam did not agonize in a slave pit; his workplace was a paradise filled with life-giving rivers, precious stones, and countless varieties of plants and animals (Gen. 2:8–14). To live in that kind of garden was a privilege; to care for it was an even greater honor. With such a magnificent blessing, how should Adam and Eve have felt about themselves?

Second, God's instruction to Adam provided a solid basis for positive self-reflection: "And the LORD God commanded the man, 'You are free to eat from any tree in the garden; but you must not eat from the tree of the knowledge of good and evil, for when you eat of it you will surely die'" (Gen. 2:16–17).

When we read this passage, its prohibition usually jumps off the page. "Why did God tell them not to eat that fruit? Why did he put Adam to the test?" we ask ourselves. These are important questions, but they easily distract us from the other side of these verses. God also gave his image tremendous freedom. He told Adam, "You are free to eat from any tree in the garden" (Gen. 2:16)—with only one exception.

Adam's liberty may not sound significant to our modern ears, but imagine how the ancient Israelites must have felt when they heard these words. In their time, the produce of a king's garden was reserved for the royal family. A common gardener would never dare to eat from it. Yet this was not the case in Eden. The King of creation gave his gardener permission to eat from all but one tree. Adam had the riches of the Creator's personal garden laid at his feet.

Third, humanity's importance in God's eyes is highlighted by the account of Eve's creation. "It is not good for the man to be alone," God said. "I will make a helper suitable for him" (Gen. 2:18). The task set before Adam was too great for him to accomplish by himself. How could one man fill the earth with images of God? How could he subdue the vast reaches of the world on his own? To help Adam fulfill these goals, God gave him a partner.

Moses repeated the word "suitable" in Genesis 2:18–20 to indicate the wonder of God's provision for Adam. Adam and his partner had to be perfect for each other. Adam searched the animal kingdom, but "no suitable helper was found" (Gen. 2:20). So God made Eve from Adam's side and brought her to him. Adam was so overwhelmed by Eve that he sang the first song recorded in the Bible: "This is now bone of my bones and flesh of my flesh; she shall be called 'woman,' for she was taken out of man" (Gen. 2:23). Moses then commented, "The man and his wife were both naked, and they felt no shame" (Gen. 2:25).

Here was a marriage made in heaven. What a portrait of honor! Two people perfectly suited to be with each other. No conflict, no trouble, absolutely no barriers spoiled their lives together. They lived in undefiled harmony, ready to be all that God had made them to be. God thought so much of Adam and Eve that he shaped their circumstances to perfection. What more could they have wanted? By looking at each other they could see how valuable they were to God.

Moses' emphasis on the blessings given to Adam and Eve exposes the initial phase of Satan's deceptive scheme. Instead of boldly challenging Eve to rebel against her Creator, Satan first led her to dissatisfaction with the honor that God had given her. He convinced Eve to question the dignity of her condition: "Did God really say, 'You must not eat from any tree in the garden'? . . . God knows that when you eat of it your eyes will be opened" (Gen. 3:1, 5). In effect, the Serpent urged, "Look at yourself, Eve. God has kept the best from you. How can you live with yourself when God has treated you this way?"

American politicians recognize this principle of persuasion. During presidential elections, the opposition party always has a twofold strategy. They not only promote their own candidate, but also discredit the other party as much as they can. More often than not, the majority of the campaign is devoted to mudslinging. Why is so much time spent on criticizing the other party? Because people must see a need for change before they will vote for it. The public will turn to other options only after being convinced that the present situation is not good.

This is precisely how Satan dealt with Eve. So long as Eve was confident that God had honored her, she had no reason to turn from him. Consequently, the Serpent first convinced Eve that it was not good enough to be the crown of creation. Under Satan's influence, Eve looked at herself, lost sight of her wonderful design, and began to turn away from her Maker.

It's easy to look back on Adam and Eve and wonder how they could have been so blind. Couldn't they see how much God had given them? Why did they lose sight of their privileged status as God's images?

But when we look at Adam and Eve, we are also looking at ourselves. We also easily lose sight of our privileges as images of God. To be sure, we do not live in a paradise, but the blessings of God still surround us. He sustains an orderly universe, shows patience toward us when we sin, provides the necessities of life, and grants a measure of prosperity and luxury to many. Nevertheless, we often find so little honor in his kindnesses that we turn away from God and pursue the poisonous fruit of sin.

Unbelievers fall prey to this temptation in innumerable ways. Sin so deceives people who are without Christ that they easily overlook God's grace toward them. The gifts of health, family, and employment are considered commonplace, not grounds for gratitude to God. What is the result of this deception? It is the same for unbelievers as it was for Eve. They do not appreciate the dignity God affords them. So they search the paths of evil for significance.

Satan's deception takes many forms in the Christian life as well. We forget the glory of forgiveness and the privilege of adoption as God's children. We lose sight even of our wondrous resurrection life in Christ. Robbed of the assurance that we are God's special treasures, we search for other things to make us feel noble.

Many times Christians compare their lives with others and wonder about their dignity. "Look at that guy," we say to ourselves. "He's got everything going for him. If I am so special, why don't I have as much as he does?" During severe trials and suffering, this kind of attitude is understandable. Even the psalmist looked at his life and cried, "I am a worm and not a man" (Ps. 22:6). But we must be careful not to feel dishonored simply because we do not have all the luxuries others enjoy.

When tempted in this way, we need to hold firmly to the precious teaching of Scripture. Christ has given each of us so many blessings that we have no reason to question our value. Christ rose on high and gave gifts to his church (Eph. 4:7–8). In so doing, he has assigned an honorable stewardship to each of us. Some blessings may seem greater than others because they are more visible, but all of Christ's gifts are gracious benevolences. He grants his Spirit to all of his people; he assures us of his presence now and an immeasurable heavenly reward in the future. With these gifts abounding in our lives, we should be fully convinced of our privileged status.

Christians also lose a sense of dignity by concentrating too much on their failures. All of us need correction and encouragement to be more obedient. When we stray far from Christ, we need sharp rebuke. But a steady diet of judgment and correction—"holy wormism," I call it—leaves us believing a deceptive lie. We confuse humility with self-degradation. We see ourselves as good-for-nothing, miserable, detestable worms, not as highly prized, redeemed images of the Creator.

Let's not lose sight of our shortcomings, but let's not lose sight of our value in God's eyes, either. Christians are coheirs with Christ (Rom. 8:17); he calls us his friends (John 15:15); we are members of his body (Eph. 5:29–30); he cherishes us as his bride (Eph. 5:23, 25; Rev. 21:9). Does that sound like we are worthless worms?

Many Christians feel uncomfortable with affirming

43

their value before God. Fearing self-aggrandizement, they run from every positive feeling about themselves. As pious as this outlook may seem, it leads us into serious danger. Failing to acknowledge the honor God has given us leads directly to the path of rebellion. Satan is looking for ways to rob us of our sense of dignity just as he stole it from Eve. When he succeeds, he has us right where he wants us. We're ready to look elsewhere for fulfillment. We're ready to do just what Eve did.

For example, what causes us to fall into the sin of greed? First, we become dissatisfied with what we have. The bank account is too low; the old car is an embarrassment; we don't think our house is nice enough. We feel that we deserve more and we go after it. What leads to marital infidelity? More often than not, adultery begins with dissatisfaction at home. We stop acknowledging the privilege of our marriage. We no longer view our spouse and children as gifts from God. Once we have lost a sense of joy in our marriage, the door is open to search for it in the arms of another.

Instead of constantly emphasizing our failures and needs, we must gain a firm conviction of our value in God's eyes. When we are fully convinced of the honor God has lavished on us in Christ, we will serve him with enthusiasm. But when we forget what God has done, we are doomed to rebel against him.

Up to this point, we have seen only one side of the Serpent's manipulation of Eve's pride. Now take a look at the second level of his strategy. Once Satan had caused Eve to lose confidence in her dignity, he led her into arrogant defiance of God. But even this aspect of his temptation was deceptive.

If someone offered you a plate of poison, would you eat it? Probably not. You would refuse pancakes sprinkled with cyanide even if you were starving. You would push aside a glass of antifreeze, no matter how thirsty you were. "I don't care what you say," you would insist. "I can tell this stuff is poison!"

Adam and Eve were also smart enough to refuse an offer of poison. The Serpent recognized this. So he did not say, "Come on Eve, eat this fruit even though it will kill you." Instead, he coaxed her into thinking that the fruit was good for her: "You will not surely die. . . . For God knows that when you eat of it your eyes will be opened, and you will be like God, knowing good and evil" (Gen. 3:4–5).

God had warned Adam that eating from the tree of the knowledge of good and evil would kill him (Gen. 2:17). But Satan told Eve, "You will be like God, knowing good and evil." Eve ate from the tree only when she was convinced that the forbidden fruit would give her the honor for which she longed as God's image.

The Evil One continues with this strategy today. He tricks us into sin by convincing us that it is good for us. How many of us lie *because* we realize that lying will destroy our lives? How many Christians break the Sabbath day *because* it wears us down to work seven days a week? If we believe an action will hurt us, we generally avoid it. Why then do we succumb to sinful actions that inevitably devastate us? We become convinced that the sin will benefit us in some way. We believe it will at least make life more bearable. Even if we know that certain behaviors will cost us in the end, we convince ourselves that the immediate benefits outweigh the eventual harm.

This kind of deception confronts us on every side. Television, movies, books, and magazines tell us that traditional Christian values are restricting and dehumanizing. Sexual promiscuity is portrayed as a positive experience among consenting adults. Greed yields the benefit of wealth. Divorce leads to personal freedom. In the end, we come to believe that wrong is right and right is wrong. Then we pursue sin for its benefits and encourage others to do the same.

How do we come to believe these lies? We do it in the same way that Eve came to believe that the forbidden fruit was good. Notice what she did just before she ate: "When

45

the woman saw that the fruit of the tree was good for food and pleasing to the eye, and also desirable for gaining wisdom, she took some and ate it. She also gave some to her husband, who was with her, and he ate it" (Gen. 3:6). Eve made her own analysis of the fruit. "I don't care what anybody says," she must have thought. "I'll check out this fruit for myself." Eve turned to the tree and examined it with her own eyes. She ate only when she had convinced herself by her own investigation that the tree was "good for food and pleasing to the eye, and also desirable for gaining wisdom" (Gen. 3:6).

We easily miss the significance of this turn of events because we live in an age that encourages us to explore the world for ourselves. Parents teach children to investigate life carefully. Scientific advances demonstrate the value of creative experimentation and discovery. From this point of view, it looks as if Eve merely used her God-given talents and searched out the options before her as well as she could.

While there is a kernel of truth here, Eve did not simply use her abilities. She misused her abilities. Instead of employing her reason in conscious submission to the word of her Creator, she set herself up as the ultimate judge. She determined for herself what to do with the fruit despite the revelation of God.

Now we see how the temptation toward false pride is so effective. Most people do not consciously shake their fist in God's face and jump into Satan's ranks. Few people intentionally cut a deal with the Devil. In most cases, people have good intentions. "I can see for myself that this is a good choice," we say. "It will *help me* if I cheat." Or, "I *need* a divorce." Or, "Abortion is my *best option.*" But in reality we have already turned away from the truth by relying on our own powers of discernment instead of God's Word.

When I was about seven years old, the boys in my neighborhood built model cars and raced them down my driveway. Most of them were a few years older than I, and they built great cars. The paint looked authentic; all the parts were in just the right places; their cars rolled fast and far. When I made my first model car, I spent a whole weekend putting it together for Monday's race. But when I went outside early in the morning, it wouldn't move. I pushed it again and again, but it simply would not roll. During the night, glue had seeped into the wheels and frozen them solid.

I ran into the house in tears and called for my mother. "My car won't roll! My car won't roll!" I cried.

Then she asked, "Did you follow the instructions?"

"The instructions?" I responded. "I don't need to read the instructions!"

But her response was to the point. "I doubt that you know how to put a car together better than the manufacturer."

She had me pegged. I was the kind of boy who never read instructions. I thought it was a mark of genius to have four or five pieces left over when I built a model. But the reality was that I did not know better than the manufacturer. I was confident in my own ability, but that confidence was false.

Eve did the same thing in Eden. God told her that eating the fruit would bring death, but Eve presumed that she did not need the instructions of the Creator. She could make the right decision on her own. And what was the outcome of her choice? Who knew better—Eve or the Manufacturer? As Scripture tells us, the fruit was poisonous after all; it brought humanity under a sentence of death.

For generations, people have imitated Adam and Eve's arrogance. Despite the countless problems we have brought on ourselves, we still set up human wisdom as the ultimate criterion of truth. But where has human insight divorced from God's revelation taken us? How well have we done through the millennia? Repeatedly our choices have led to ruin. Look at the testimony of history. Great accomplishments are but brief respites from the oppression, injustice, and destruction that dominate our past. When we are honest with ourselves, we must acknowledge that our false pride has destroyed us.

By looking at the first temptation, we can learn a lot about ourselves. Satan also tricks us by playing with our pride. He first robs us of legitimate pride in the honor God has given us. Then he leads us to pursue false pride. We turn away from God and decide that we can discover on our own how to make life worth living. Yet, as in the Garden of Eden, our decision causes us to sink into ruin.

THE TURN TOWARD RUIN

A few months ago, I was driving to a retreat center in rural Florida. The sun was going down and time was growing short. "It's thirty minutes before I speak," I thought to myself as I raced to get there on time. But after twenty minutes had passed, I was completely lost. I pulled into a gas station and asked for help.

"No problem," a young man assured me. "You only made one wrong turn."

"Great!" I replied. "That's not so bad."

But then he smiled and said, "Yeah, it was just one turn, but it was an hour back down the road!" Needless to say, I didn't make it to the conference on time. It was just one wrong turn, but that mistake had led me far from my destination.

Adam and Eve made a wrong turn in Eden by eating the forbidden fruit. It was just one act of disobedience, but it has taken all of us far from our original destiny. What were the results of their sin? How has their rebellion affected the human race?

God had warned Adam, "When you eat of [the fruit] you will surely die" (Gen. 2:17), and his warning came true. God drove Adam and Eve from the garden, cutting them off from the tree of life (Gen. 3:23–24). Spiritual death came immediately; like a rushing tidal wave, it destroyed humanity's moral rectitude. God's image became "dead in . . . transgressions and sins" (Eph. 2:1). From that point on, we had no good in ourselves. Every human being after that came into the world spiritually and morally dead.

Physical death also came to Adam and Eve. Human existence began to be characterized by suffering, disease, and pain. Life for the image of God was reduced to little more than prolonged dying.

Many people today hear this biblical portrait of life and scoff. "My life isn't that bad. I'm doing just fine," they say. We have to admit that many people enjoy fine health and live the good life. If this is so, how can we say that sin has ruined the human race? Isn't Moses' portrait a bit exaggerated?

If we look closely, it soon becomes evident that Moses' account is quite accurate. Many unbelievers have simply covered themselves with a veneer of happiness. They appear to be unaffected by sin; they seem to have it all together. But beneath the facade of success, unbelievers hardly measure up to their claims. Turning from God has reduced them to a cheap imitation of what they claim to be.

What have been the results of our rebellion against God? Let's answer this question by looking at two things: what sin *has not* done and what it *has* done.

In the first place, we must see what sin *has not* done to the human race. Put simply, the fall of humanity has not reduced us to beasts. People remain the image of God despite their failures. We may not live as God's likenesses should, but every person—no matter how wicked or vile—is still the visible image of God in the world.

Two passages of Scripture indicate clearly that all people remain the image of God. After the flood, God spoke these words to Noah: "Whoever sheds the blood of man, by man shall his blood be shed; for in the image of God has God made man" (Gen. 9:6). Murder is punishable by legal execution because everyone, including those who rebel against God, are images of God.

A similar passage appears in the New Testament. James 3:9–10 reads: "With the tongue we praise our Lord and Father, and with it we curse men, who have been made in God's likeness. Out of the same mouth come praise and cursing. My brothers, this should not be." This instruction is not limited to our treatment of fellow believers. James calls us to treat all human beings as the image of God.

How do fallen people remain the image of God? In what ways are they still God's likeness? First, people possess many basic characteristics granted to Adam and Eve in the beginning. We exhibit rational and linguistic capacities; we have moral and religious natures; we are immortal souls. Sin severely mars these aspects of our character, but it does not obliterate them.

Second, fallen people remain God's image in that they are still required to multiply and have dominion. After the Flood, God reiterated to all humanity the mandate originally given to Adam and Eve: "Then God blessed Noah and his sons, saying to them, 'Be fruitful and increase in number and fill the earth. The fear and dread of you will fall upon all the beasts of the earth and all the birds of the air, upon every creature that moves along the ground, and upon all the fish of the sea; they are given into your hands'" (Gen. 9:1–2). Noah and his sons were sinners, but God insisted that they continue in their original calling as his image. Sin has seriously impacted all dimensions of these tasks, but we are still responsible for them. God expects all people in all places to multiply and have dominion.

Whatever else we may say about fallen humanity, we must remember that we remain the image of God. We have rebelled against our Maker, but we are still people. All of us are special creations designed with marvelous abilities and blessed with unique responsibilities in this world.

In the second place, however, we must also recognize what sin *has* done to the human race. We are fallen, corrupted images of God. Disobedience against God has so ruined humanity that we are in need of extensive renovation.

In the third chapter of Genesis, Moses acknowledged humanity's corruption in two ways. First, he pointed to the scarring of our moral character. After eating the fruit, Adam and Eve were overwhelmed with guilt. Their peace with God was so disrupted that they hid themselves. When God called to Adam, he answered, "I heard you in the garden, and I was afraid because I was naked; so I hid" (Gen. 3:10). Originally, Adam and Eve were naked without shame (Gen. 2:25). They enjoyed open harmony with each other and God. Now, however, they recognized that they were no longer holy and righteous; they were morally defiled.

The rest of Scripture teaches that sin has affected every dimension of human character. We are totally depraved. To be sure, we are not as bad as we could be. God restrains sin and enables us to avoid absolute ruin. When left to our own devices, however, we are utterly corrupted in all our faculties. Our thinking processes are so darkened that we twist and pervert the truth (1 Cor. 2:14; John 1:5; Rom. 8:7; Eph. 4:18; Titus 1:15). Our wills have been rendered unable to choose what is spiritually good (John 8:34; 2 Tim. 3:2–4). Our affections have been marred and misdirected so that we love the world and its evil pleasures (John 5:42; Heb. 3:12; 1 John 2:15–17). For these reasons, we are under the judgment of God (John 3:18–19) and unable to do anything to redeem ourselves (John 6:44; 3:5; Rom. 7:18, 23). The sin of Adam and Eve has had a devastating effect on human character.

Second, Moses taught that sin left its mark on our calling as God's image. God cursed Adam and Eve precisely in the areas most central to their lives: multiplication and dominion. Consider God's word to the woman: "I will greatly increase your pains in childbearing; with pain you will give birth to children. Your desire will be for your husband, and he will rule over you" (Gen. 3:16). Eve faced a

51

terrible curse on childbearing and marriage. She would continue in marriage and have children, but now both aspects of her life were corrupted.

On the one hand, the harmony between Adam and Eve was disrupted: "Your desire will be for your husband, and he will rule over you." Hostility replaced the unity and cooperation that existed before the Fall. Instead of being a source of strength, marriage became an arena of trouble and conflict.

On the other hand, God addressed the bearing and raising of children: "I will greatly increase your pains in childbearing." The glorious privilege of producing images of God became a painful burden. It would now take place with suffering.

Usually, we limit this curse to the physical discomfort of giving birth. Labor pain is certainly in view here; children come into the world inflicting physical suffering on their mothers. Nevertheless, the pain of which God spoke in Genesis 3:16 also has the connotation of emotional suffering. Suffering associated with children does not end with their birth. Children inflict grief on their mothers throughout their lives.

A few years ago, I suggested to a group of women that children bring emotional pain to their parents. Afterwards, I overheard two of them talking. "I don't know what he means," the younger woman objected. "My little girl brings me joy, not pain."

"How old is your daughter?" the older woman asked.

"Six weeks," said the first.

Then the older woman smiled and replied, "Just wait until she's sixteen."

Children are wonderful gifts from God, but these precious rewards now also cause us grief. As the years go by, our youngsters disappoint us; sometimes they reject us and everything we hold dear. Eve certainly experienced this kind of sorrow when her son Cain murdered his own brother.

The history of the world can be written in terms of the tears that mothers have shed over their children. So many mothers work hard to discipline their children, only to see them rebel. They pour their lives into their little ones, only to lose them to the carelessness of a drunk driver. They devote endless hours to teaching them about Christ, only to see them pursue the ways of death. All loving parents must bear disappointment and sorrow from their children; our sin brought this curse upon us.

In the previous chapter, we saw that one way in which we multiply is by reaching the lost for Christ. This dimension of multiplication is also cursed with pain. Spiritual mothers and fathers face many frustrations with their children in Christ. What pastor has not seen church members wander from the faith? Anyone involved in reaching out to others will find similar trials. Advice goes unheeded and warnings fall on deaf ears.

We were made to fill the world with likenesses of God. We must continue to carry out that task by giving birth, raising children in Christ, and bringing the lost to the Savior. But how the magnificent image of God has fallen! Now our task is corrupted by severe pain and futility.

After pronouncing his curse on Eve, God turned to Adam. At this point he focused on our call to exercise dominion: "Cursed is the ground because of you; through painful toil you will eat of it all the days of your life. It will produce thorns and thistles for you, and you will eat the plants of the field. By the sweat of your brow you will eat your food until you return to the ground, since from it you were taken; for dust you are and to dust you will return" (Gen. 3:17–19). God's words revealed at once that humanity still had the responsibility of ruling over the earth. Nevertheless, Adam's task was now full of suffering.

God declared that Adam's work would be plagued with difficulty: "Through painful toil you will eat of [the ground] all the days of your life" (Gen. 3:17). Before the Fall, the ground freely yielded its bounty, but now it offers vigorous resistance. In many ways, the world became hostile to human life. Under the curse of God, Adam had to struggle just to survive.

I have never met a person who has not experienced Adam's struggle for survival. Some people experience it more bitterly than others. Young couples work and work, but find the bills piling higher and higher. Retirees cannot make ends meet on their fixed incomes. Even those who are financially successful face other difficulties in their lives. They may live in fine homes, drive expensive cars, and belong to the best country clubs, but other aspects of their lives fall apart right before their eyes.

The curse on Adam did not stop with pain and struggle. God declared a bitter fate for his image. Adam would work endlessly, wrestling day and night against the forces of nature. But to what end? A glorious victory over futility? Hardly. God declared, "By the sweat of your brow you will eat your food until you return to the ground, since from it you were taken; for dust you are and to dust you will return" (Gen. 3:19). In short, Adam would work himself to death.

We have heard this verse so many times that we easily gloss over its powerful imagery. This passage is much more than an abstract theological explanation of death. It is God speaking to his image—his once perfect, glorious image. This was Adam, whom God carefully shaped from the dust and into whom he breathed life. Now this same Adam would die and return to the dust.

A friend shared a dream with me that relates to the imagery of this passage. Her mother had recently passed away, and one evening her mind wandered to thoughts of her. "At first she was a sight to behold," she told me. "She looked so young and strong." As she continued, however, a tear came to her eye. "Suddenly, I saw her buried in the graveyard. Before I knew it, her face began to shrink; her flesh rotted away before my eyes. Her skeleton disintegrated into dust." Her description was horrifying. "Then I realized something," she concluded. "It wouldn't be long before I was there, too."

How we run from this horrible reality! From day to day we do our very best to forget the inevitability of death. Just look at men and women as they rush to work each morning. They push and shove into the elevator as if they were on the way to doing something that will last forever. How much are they thinking about the cold graves that wait for them? How conscious are they of the vanity of success? How aware are they of the brevity of life? Most people refuse to contemplate their end. Death is the furthest thing from their minds. People live in the here and now, in the moment at hand, running from the reality of futility and death.

But we cannot run forever. We may try to escape the tragedy of death for a while, but reality eventually breaks through. A loved one passes away; we read the obituary of a friend. Suddenly we realize where we are all going.

I wish we could pass over the horror of death. I wish we did not have to deal with it at all, but let's not fool ourselves. Death does not go away when we ignore it. We must face the terrible reality of the grave.

This harsh reality has driven many people to utter despair. "If I'm just going to turn back into dust," they say, "what's the use in living?" But a positive result can come from staring into our gaping caskets. Peering into the face of death is the starting point for rising above the ruin that Adam and Eve brought on the human race. When we finally realize what awaits us, we see how much we need to be rescued. We long for the grace of God to deliver us from our misery.

Is there hope for God's image? Can we ever escape the suffering caused by our rebellion? God did not leave Adam and Eve without hope of rescue. He did not desert them to the futility of sin's harsh dominion. Instead, he offered us hope—hope that we will one day rise above this futility.

Even as God pronounced severe curses on his image,

he also spoke of a brighter future: "And I will put enmity between you and the woman, and between your offspring and hers; he will crush your head, and you will strike his heel" (Gen. 3:15). These words revealed God's plan for humanity. We will have victory over Satan. The Serpent would continue to trouble Eve's descendants, constantly nipping at their heels, but one day the children of Eve would crush Satan's head in glorious victory.

The New Testament tells us that this wonderful destiny is ultimately realized in Jesus Christ, the greatest child of Eve. In his death, Christ severely limited the power of Satan. "Since the children have flesh and blood, he too shared in their humanity so that by his death he might destroy him who holds the power of death—that is, the devil" (Heb. 2:14).

When Christ rose from the dead, he gained victory over death and the grave. "'Death has been swallowed up in victory.' 'Where, O death, is your victory? Where, O death, is your sting?' The sting of death is sin, and the power of sin is the law. But thanks be to God! He gives us the victory through our Lord Jesus Christ" (1 Cor. 15:54–57). The final victory over Satan and over the curse of death will occur when God's redeemed people inherit the new heavens and the new earth. As Paul told the Christians at Rome, "The God of peace will soon crush Satan under your feet" (Rom. 16:20). Christ will lead us to glory even as Adam led us into death.

Although many centuries passed before the promise given to Adam and Eve began to be fulfilled in Christ, God never utterly abandoned the human race to the horrors of futility and death. Throughout the history of the Bible, God paved a way for his fallen images to receive foretastes of the dignity Christ would give to his people. He granted rich blessings in the days of Noah, Abraham, Moses, and David, which lifted his people above the horrible tyranny of sin and death. As we learn about these blessings and lay hold of them by faith, we can find relief from the curses placed on

Adam and Eve. We can see Satan and sin defeated here and now.

There is good news for those who look into their graves. The search for redemption is not in vain. Out of love and compassion, God constructed a road that leads to the restoration of humanity. It is a wondrous path that brings us to ever greater blessings of dignity as images of God (see Figure 3).

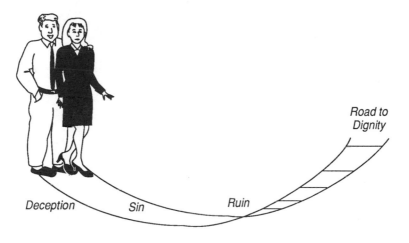

Figure 3. Sinking of Humanity

CONCLUSION

In this chapter we have looked at the familiar biblical account of humanity's fall into sin. We noticed that Adam and Eve sank into ruin because they lost sight of their honor as God's images and foolishly became arrogant before God. It was just one turn of events, one sinful act, but the defiance of the first man and woman brought curses on the whole human race. Look at what we made of ourselves. The wondrous likeness of God cast itself into a sea of futility and death. In the chapters that follow we will see how God rescued his image and restored us to dignity.

꒳   ꒳   ꒳

REVIEW QUESTIONS

1. What were the two aspects of Satan's deceptive strategy against Eve? How can we avoid his deception in our own lives?
2. What *did not* happen to Adam and Eve as a result of their sin? What *did* happen to them as a result of their rebellion against God?
3. What were the effects of sin on humanity's calling to multiply and exercise dominion? Why should we face these terrible aspects of human existence?

DISCUSSION EXERCISES

1. Why is this chapter entitled "Sinking into Ruin"?
2. Describe one person you know who has lost all positive self-esteem. Describe another person who is full of arrogant self-importance. Why are both of these people in dangerous positions? Which danger do you face in your life?
3. Take a look at your own experience of multiplication. List five ways in which you suffer pain in your attempts to multiply God's image. What hope is there for you in Christ?
4. List five ways in which you suffer futility in your attempts to exercise dominion over the earth. What hope is there for you in Christ?

4

TURNING AROUND

Several hundred students crowded the inner-city high school gym on the first day of class. Shouts of laughter filled the air as the principal called the meeting to order. "This year is your chance to turn your life around," he began. At first, the students rolled their eyes at each other. "Here we go again," they whispered. "Another pep talk."

But the principal's next words caused a hush to come over the crowd. "This summer, two of our tenth graders died in gang violence," he said. "What will happen to the rest of you? . . . We're giving you a chance to be somebody, but you have to take advantage of the opportunity."

That school principal understood his students well. He realized how easily they fell prey to the corruption and violence surrounding them. He was determined to give his students a chance at a better life, but they still had to take advantage of their opportunity.

As we will see in this chapter, every human being faces this kind of situation. We may not reside in crime-infested neighborhoods, but we all live in a world that threatens to destroy us. Nevertheless, long ago in the days of Noah, God intervened in history and made it possible for humanity to rise above the ruinous effects of evil. He gave us the opportunity to turn our lives around, but it is still our responsibility to do something with that opportunity.

OUR THREATENING SITUATION

The biblical account of Noah's flood is a popular children's story. Look in any church nursery; peek into the baby's room of any Christian home. You'll find at least one symbol related to Noah—an ark, a rainbow, a pair of giraffes. We smile when we think about the "Doctor Doolittle" of the Bible.

Unfortunately, we associate this part of the Bible so much with children that we often forget that it has a serious adult message. Noah's story is not just for little people. It challenges us to reflect on the threatening situation that evil has brought to us. As we saw in the previous chapter, Adam and Eve brought the human race under a severe curse, but the degradation of humanity did not stop there. It only increased when Adam and Eve had their first children.

The story of Cain and Abel is well known (Gen. 4:1–16). Both men offered sacrifices to God: Cain brought leftovers from his field (v. 3), and Abel offered "the firstborn of his flock" (v. 4). God rejected Cain's hypocritical offering, but he accepted Abel's sincere sacrifice. As a result, Cain was filled with jealousy and murdered Abel (v. 8).

How could Cain have done this? What caused the glorious image of God to degenerate to the point of committing fratricide? Isn't this just the opposite of what God made us to be? God's warning to Cain revealed the answer. Cain lived in a threatening situation: "If you do what is right, will you not be accepted? But if you do not do what is right, sin is crouching at your door; it desires to have you, but you must master it" (v. 7). Cain's circumstances were frightful. An evil force was at work in the fallen world, actively seeking to conquer Adam's son. If Cain did not master sin, it would master him.

Most modern people have a hard time thinking of evil as an active force. If they believe in sin at all, it only amounts to the individual actions we choose for ourselves.

We laugh when we hear people say, "The Devil made me do it." "The Devil doesn't make anyone do anything!" we contend. We ignore the personal, supernatural character of evil and conclude that it's all a matter of our choices. To be sure, we choose to sin and we are responsible for our decisions. Yet, the Scriptures consistently present a more complex picture. We live in a world where evil outside of ourselves schemes to overwhelm us.

Recognizing the threat of evil is essential to overcoming the effects of sin. As long as we think that sin is merely an internal struggle—a flaw within us—we will never take it as seriously as we ought. We can manage that kind of devil. But what about a supernatural Satan with the goal of conquering and ruining us? We have to take that kind of Devil seriously. We put up our defenses and form our counterstrategies. We work hard to master sin before it masters us.

"It's a dog-eat-dog world," we often say to each other. "If you don't win, someone else will." These words ring true in many areas of life, especially in sports and business. But the story of Cain tells us that all of life is a competition with supernatural evil. Evil does not sit quietly. Either we conquer it or it conquers us.

What was the result of Cain's failure? Did sin's dominion benefit or harm him?

I have several friends in the armed forces. Like all soldiers, they have moved from base to base over the years. I asked one fellow how he liked moving so much. "It all depends on the commanding officers," he explained. "If the commanders are good, the move is good. If they're bad, the move can be terrible."

Military officers have a lot of power over the lives of the men and women under them. They can make life pleasant or miserable. It all depends on the kind of people they are.

The events before Noah's flood reveal what kind of commander sin is. First, when Cain submitted to sin's mastery, it did not benefit him. Sin was a horrible master; it turned Cain into a monstrous murderer.

Second, the genealogy of Cain (Gen. 4:17–24) demonstrates what sin does to us the longer we remain under its dominion. It ends with the song of Lamech: "Adah and Zillah, listen to me; wives of Lamech, hear my words. I have killed a man for wounding me, a young man for injuring me. If Cain is avenged seven times, then Lamech seventy-seven times" (Gen. 4:23–24). Lamech was a murderer like Cain, but he went beyond his ancestor by actually taking pride in his horrible crime. He sang to his wives of murdering a young man.

Every murder is terrible, but we are especially horrified when killers boast of their brutalities. "What kind of person could do such a thing?" we ask ourselves. This is precisely the reaction Moses wanted his readers to have toward Lamech. His arrogant song revealed how sin continued to defile God's image. We plummeted so far under the influence of evil that we not only killed, but took pleasure in it. We began to enjoy inflicting pain on our fellow human beings.

A bit of relief from these depressing events appears in Genesis 4:25–5:32, which traces the line of Seth, Adam's third son. This family tree included people who would "call on the name of the LORD" (Gen. 4:26). They were special images of God, resisting the corruption of sin and faithfully serving God. But the positive note sounded by Seth's descendants quickly disappears in the cacophony of the sixth chapter of Genesis.

In Genesis 6:1–8, Moses recorded a third example of sin's mastery over God's image. "The sons of God" forcibly took "daughters of men" in marriage. Biblical interpreters disagree over precisely who these characters were. Some believe that the passage refers to angels ("sons of God") who married human women ("daughters of men"). Others see a reference to intermarriage between Sethite men and Cainite women. Still others think that the story depicts evil kings and princes taking women of common birth and forcing them to be their wives. We cannot be sure of the precise identities of these characters, but one thing is clear: these marriages were an expression of abuse and violence.

At the end of this series of events, God surveyed the human race and took note of how extensively sin had defiled us: "The LORD saw how great man's wickedness on the earth had become, and that every inclination of the thoughts of his heart was only evil all the time" (Gen. 6:5).

Adam and Eve turned away from God, Cain murdered his brother, Lamech boasted of his barbarism, and a race of oppressors was formed. As history took its course, defilement and degradation became the natural course for our race. Evil completely filled the human heart.

These stories of early human history alert us to two horrible truths about us all. First, sin still does not lie dormant. It is on the prowl, desiring to master you and me. Second, it is rare that we resist. Just as early humanity spiraled downward, so the vast majority of the human race today is overwhelmed by sin's power.

Think about how natural it is for you to rebel against God. Consider how easily you come under sin's influence. We do not have to devise ways to turn away from God. We do not have to plan on it. All we have to do is drop our guard and sin inflicts its damaging blows.

For example, what do you have to do to ruin your family? What is required to obliterate the bonds that hold your home together? In our fallen world, simply let nature take its course. Sin will prevail and your family will be destroyed.

What do you have to do to grow cold in your relationship with Christ? What must you do to ruin your walk with him? You don't have to do anything. Sin still seeks to master you, and if you don't consciously resist it, your walk with Christ will grow ice cold.

This principle is not true only for individuals. It also applies corporately. The natural tendency of every nation is to move further under the destructive power of sin. Consider, for instance, the legalization of abortion in Western nations. Those created for the honor of reproducing images of God now mercilessly murder them in the womb. But the decline of nations will not stop here. If we abort our unborn today, what savagery will we inflict in a generation or two on others who have no voice? The nightmares of euthanasia for the weak and elderly are not far away. Sin aggressively seeks to control us and drive us away from the enrichment of human dignity. Apart from God's grace, evil will always overwhelm us and bring us dishonor.

The utter horror of sin's mastery becomes plain in God's reaction to the human race. He was not mildly displeased with his image; he was utterly grieved: "The LORD was grieved that he had made man on the earth, and his heart was filled with pain. So the LORD said, 'I will wipe mankind, whom I have created, from the face of the earth—men and animals, and creatures that move along the ground, and birds of the air—for I am grieved that I have made them'" (Gen. 6:6–7). What a disheartening scene. God actually regretted having made us. His images had so radically departed from their original state that they belonged in the trash heap.

Take a look at your children. Remember the times when you lovingly cuddled them in your arms. Now ask yourself a question. What would your children have to do for you to say, "I'm sorry I had them"? How evil would they have to become before you would destroy them? It's unimaginable, isn't it? But God openly declared that the men and women he had made in his likeness were so corrupt, so utterly defiled, that they had to be destroyed.

"But surely we don't see this degree of degradation today," we think to ourselves. "People are doing much better now." But take another look. What made God so angry in the days of Noah? Moses tells us: "Now the earth was corrupt in God's sight and was full of violence. God saw how corrupt the earth had become, for all the people on earth had corrupted their ways. So God said to Noah, 'I am going to put an end to all people, for the earth is filled with violence because of them. I am surely going to destroy both them and the earth'" (Gen. 6:11–13).

The key word in this passage is "violence." We know that God was angry with humanity because sin was an affront to his holiness, but how did this defiance manifest itself on earth? The human race covered the world with a sea of violence. Sin displayed its mastery over humanity in the form of strife, hatred, and abuse.

Have we overcome the violence that stirred the wrath of God in the days of Noah? It isn't hard to find the answer to this question.

Imagine you are an extraterrestrial hovering over planet Earth. Your job is to monitor television and radio signals in order to learn about the human race. What characteristics stand out? What report will you make to your superiors?

As you listen to the news and observe popular television shows, it won't be long before you draw a firm conclusion. "Let's get out of here!" you shout to your captain. "These human beings are the most violent creatures in the universe!"

We are preoccupied with violence. Watch a group of toddlers playing; after a few minutes one will hit or push the other. Children's favorite cartoons feature martial arts experts and intergalactic warriors. Gangs of adolescents roam the streets robbing and raping. They entertain themselves with slasher films highlighting unspeakable brutalities. Parents physically abuse their children. Husbands batter their wives. Totalitarian governments imprison and torture political opponents. Nations threaten each other with chemical warfare and nuclear annihilation.

All of the violence in our world confirms that we are just like the people living in Noah's time. Sin still masters the human race today, and we still deserve the judgment of God. In fact, the Scriptures teach that a day of judgment is coming. This time it will not be a judgment of water but of fire: "But they deliberately forget that long ago by God's word the heavens existed and the earth was formed out of water and by water. By these waters also the world of that time was deluged and destroyed. By the same word the present heavens and earth are reserved for fire, being kept for the day of judgment and destruction of ungodly men" (2 Peter 3:5–7).

Until that day, all of us must recognize our threatening situation. Evil plots our defeat and we easily fall prey to its vicious mastery. Left to our own devices, we will not pursue choices that enrich our existence as God's images. We will always subject ourselves to the degradation of sin's power. We become so much the opposite of our original design that we deserve to be destroyed.

OUR OPPORTUNITY

During the Christmas season two years ago, we had a disastrous freeze in central Florida. When the cold weather passed, my wife and I noticed that one of our beautiful tropical plants had withered. We asked a friend what we should do. "Cut off everything and just leave the stump," he told us.

"But won't that kill the whole thing?" I objected.

"No," he explained, "cutting off the dead branches will give it a chance to live."

Following our friend's advice, we hired a student to take care of the tree. When I first saw the remains of our plant, I couldn't believe my eyes. We had only a tiny mangled stump left. I was sure there was no hope for recovery, but in just a few weeks some signs of new life appeared. As the weather improved, the plant continued to flourish. Now, the tree has grown bigger than it was before the freeze.

In the days of Noah, God stripped the human race of its withered branches. He cut us back to the stump of just one man and his family by sending a flood. This judgment was severe, but it was done with a positive end in mind. Through his radical judgment, God made it possible for the human race to thrive once again. He gave us the opportunity to overcome the degradation of sin.

We get the first hint of God's positive purpose in the Flood when Noah received his name from his father. Noah's father was a man of faith from the line of Seth. He chose the name Noah and explained, "He will comfort us in the labor and painful toil of our hands caused by the ground the LORD has cursed" (Gen. 5:29).

To appreciate these words, we have to understand that the name Noah is related to the Hebrew word often translated "comfort," "rest," or "relief." Noah's father hoped that his son would bring comfort and rest to the world. But what kind of comfort was Noah to bring? He would bring rest from the curse of futility imposed on humanity in the garden. "Cursed is the ground because of you," God declared to Adam (Gen. 3:17). Through Noah, however, God was giving a measure of relief from "the labor and painful toil . . . caused by the ground the LORD has cursed" (Gen. 5:29).

When the Scriptures say that Noah would "comfort us," they do not mean that he would eliminate all pain and futility from the world. So long as death continued to be part of human experience, the curse remained. Nevertheless, God did something magnificent through Noah to counter the curse placed on humanity. Noah was the first major step in God's plan to redeem the fallen race. He was the first milestone on the long road to dignity for the image of God.

What did God accomplish in Noah's day? What kind of comfort and relief did he provide? We can understand what God did by joining Noah as he comes out of the ark.

The door of the ark opens and the animals begin to emerge. Look around yourself and see the devastation left by the Flood. All of civilization is gone—the cultivated fields, the homes, the schools, the great cities. What must have been racing through Noah's mind? "If this is what God does to us when we sin, there's no use in building again. After so many days cooped up in that ark, I know that my sons and I are still sinners. We will fail again. Why should we try to rebuild if God is just going to destroy us?"

We can have confidence that Noah wondered these things when we see what God thought to himself after Noah offered his sacrifice:

> The LORD smelled the pleasing aroma and said in his heart: "Never again will I curse the ground because of man, even though every inclination of his heart is evil from childhood. And never again will I destroy all living creatures, as I have done. As long as the earth endures, seedtime and harvest, cold and heat, summer and winter, day and night will never cease." (Gen. 8:21–22)

God promised to provide an orderly and predictable place for his image "as long as the earth endures" (v. 22). He granted Noah and his sons a world of regular cycles— "seedtime and harvest, cold and heat, summer and winter, day and night" (v. 22). Calamities would still intrude into human life from time to time; storms and floods would come. But total devastation by water would never take place again. The order of nature would be secure until the end of history.

To confirm his word, God put a sign in the sky: "And God said, '. . . I have set my rainbow in the clouds, and it will be the sign of the covenant between me and the earth. . . . Never again will the waters become a flood to destroy all life. Whenever the rainbow appears in the clouds, I will see it and remember the everlasting covenant between God and all living creatures of every kind on the earth'" (Gen. 9:12–16).

In this passage God revealed the symbolic meaning of the rainbow. The Hebrew word rendered "rainbow" in many modern translations may be translated "bow," the ordinary instrument of war. The only qualification in the original language is that God called it "my bow." In other words, the rainbow is God's heavenly bow, his instrument of war. Just as bolts of lightning served as God's arrows (cf. Ps. 18:14), so the rainbow served as God's weapon of destruction.

The bow of God had powerful significance in Noah's time. God had just come in stormy judgment. He had destroyed humanity with his magnificent bow and arrows. Now, however, God assured Noah that he no longer targeted the human race. He promised to hang his bow in the clouds, pointed away from the earth, as a sign of peace and security. Now Noah could get on with the business of being God's image in spite of his failures. God had promised him the opportunity of a stable world.

The order of nature is a wonderful gift from God. We can see how important it is when we hear news reports of natural disasters. Think of the damage caused by a hurricane or the devastation caused by drought. If a summer is too hot or a winter too cold, the hardships can be enormous.

More than this, the regularity of nature provides God's image with the opportunity to make something out of life. It is an expression of divine patience toward us.

A pastor friend once told me about someone in his church who had little patience with his children. Whenever the kids were around, he watched their every move. If they were not absolutely perfect, he scolded them severely. "Tuck in your shirt! . . . Fix your hair! . . . Don't be so loud! . . . Speak up! . . . Sit down! . . . Stand up!" One afternoon my friend could take it no longer. "They're just kids!" he said angrily. "You've got to be patient and give them a chance to grow up."

In much the same way, God recognized the frailty of his image. He knew that "every inclination of [the human] heart is evil from childhood" (Gen. 8:21). As a result, God determined to exercise patience toward his image. Realizing that we would continue to fall short, he gave us a stable world that affords the human race time to grow up.

Throughout history, God has been faithful to this promise. He has not destroyed humanity every time wickedness has arisen. Indeed, we have failed miserably again and again, but God has graciously sustained a world of enduring order. This orderly world has become our opportunity to rise out of futility and destruction.

But how do we react to this gracious gift? How do we view the predictability and regularity of our lives? Noah saw it as a blessing, but let's face it—we usually look on it as boring. We all have a tendency to be bored with the predictability of life. The alarm goes off at the same time every morning; we drive the same car to the same office, and answer the same phone. We wash the same dishes, and change diapers on the same baby over and over. Nothing ever changes; we get tired of the same old grind, day after day.

My family and I live near Disney World, the fun capital of the world. It's been interesting to hear the reactions of our friends when they learn where we live. "Wow," one fellow said facetiously. "It must be great—sun and fun all the time!" Of course, I'm quick to let everyone know that we don't spend all of our time at tourist spots; our lives are actually very ordinary. But our friends' reactions reveal the way most of us think. "Disney World and the beach! Now that's the good life!"

Vacations are great. Recreation is an important part of God's plan for us. But we must take to heart the Bible's outlook on the regularities of life. Stability, however boring, is a blessing. The predictability of daily affairs provides an opportunity for weak and failing images of God to rise out of the mire of self-destruction. It is our opportunity to overcome.

How often do you complain about how ordinary your life is? Do you find yourself wishing that you could have a thrilling, fun-filled lifestyle like you see in the movies?

"Nothing unusual ever happens to me," we say. "Why can't things be more exciting?"

If you think that getting out of bed early every morning is a bore, then talk with someone who can't get out of bed. If you look at your job as a tiresome nuisance, then speak with someone who can't find a job. If you find yourself wondering if you can stand to change another diaper, talk to someone who cannot have children. Then you will see that these regular activities are actually opportunities for you to build a life worth living.

Isn't it wonderful that you have more than one day to train your children in the ways of Christ? Aren't you glad that you have more than one chance to make your career a success? Where would you be if you did not have an orderly world? Without stability in our lives, we would never be able to multiply God's images; we would never succeed in having dominion over the earth.

For most of us, today will be like yesterday; tomorrow will be much like today. If the Lord tarries, next year, even the next decade, will be like those in the past. Realize that this regularity of life is God's gracious gift. It is our opportunity to overcome the ruinous effects of sin.

OUR RESPONSIBILITY

When I first began to teach in seminary, I got a call from a former classmate. "You must be thrilled at the opportunity to teach," he said to me.

"Yes," I replied, "but I'm also scared."

"What do you mean?" he asked.

"This is not just an opportunity," I explained. "It's also a big responsibility."

The story of Noah also connects opportunity with responsibility. God formed the world into a stable sphere to give us opportunity. But he has called us to act responsibly in this world. After assuring Noah of regularity in life (Gen.

8:21–22), God immediately told him what his responsibility was: "Be fruitful and increase in number and fill the earth. The fear and dread of you will fall upon all the beasts of the earth and all the birds of the air, upon every creature that moves along the ground, and upon all the fish of the sea; they are given into your hands" (Gen. 9:1–2). God reaffirmed his original design for humanity by telling Noah to continue multiplying and exercising dominion.

God's command to Noah stands in opposition to the ways in which many unbelievers think. Sin so clouds their minds that they permit the regularity of life to lull them into complacency about the commands of God. They go on pursuing the ways of degradation, assuming that they have plenty of time to turn their lives around.

On a number of occasions, I have run into this brick wall in evangelistic encounters. "Don't you see your need for Christ?" I eventually ask. "Yes," the person often admits, "but I've got lots of time before I have to change my life."

Of course it is true that most people do have years to live. God probably will not whisk them away in the next few moments. But this is an utterly foolish excuse for remaining under the mastery of sin. The order that God has ordained for the universe in no way assures individuals of longevity. The sun may rise every morning for the next million years, but it may never rise on you or me again. The preservation of the natural order after the Flood should not give anyone false personal assurances. People are snatched from life without a moment's notice every day.

This is one reason why God commissioned Noah immediately after promising him an orderly universe. God knew our propensity toward spiritual procrastination. "If we have a stable world," we think to ourselves, "why not wait for a more convenient time to get our lives together?" But God short-circuited this way of thinking in Noah's life by immediately reminding him of his responsibility to serve as God's image. The preservation of nature—the sun, the seasons, the very air we breathe—is designed to give us an arena for serving God, not for ignoring his claims on our lives.

In addition, notice where God told Noah to work. He did not command him to leave the sinful world to run its own course. He did not tell him to withdraw from real life. Noah was not to fly away somewhere *over* the rainbow. He was to serve God *under* the rainbow. God called Noah to become involved in the world. "Be fruitful and increase in number" (Gen. 9:7). Noah was to continue carrying out the responsibilities originally designed for God's image. Even though the world was corrupt, God commissioned his redeemed image to work in it.

Many believers see the Christian faith as a way to escape from the world, rather than as a commission to be involved in it. You don't have to listen to many preachers on the radio or television before you hear someone say, "Don't worry about politics; don't spend time on social programs. These things are unimportant. Jesus is coming back soon to rescue us from these problems."

This view has dominated evangelical perspectives in the United States since World War II, leading most committed Christians to withdraw from public life. The sciences and arts, mass media, education, and politics have been largely left in the hands of unbelievers. "Let unbelievers take care of this corrupt world," we say. "We have our hands full just getting people on the lifeboats to heaven."

Evangelism is one of our principal responsibilities as Christians, but God has not called us to emphasize saving souls so much that we desert other dimensions of this world. We too easily become concerned with this life and fix our hopes on earthly goals. Yet, this danger should never cause us to run in the other direction. Just as God commissioned Noah to serve him in the present age, so we have been called to involve ourselves as well.

Jesus put it this way: "You are the salt of the earth. . . . You are the light of the world" (Matt. 5:13, 14). Sin is ready to extend its mastery over humanity. When the salt and light do not resist its influence, decay and darkness run rampant in the world. If you and I do not accept the responsibility given to Noah and his sons, we leave the world to suffer more and more under the cruel mastery of sin.

Where has religious escapism taken us in modern Western culture? What has been the result of our failure to serve as salt and light? Take a look at the great centers of population in the West. Europe and the United States have degenerated into Christian graveyards. The stench is overwhelming. Crime, immorality, sexual diseases, and drug abuse run rampant. Christian values are but faint memories of centuries long forgotten. This is what happens when Christians try to escape, rather than fulfill their responsibilities in the world.

Sometimes I become angry with the direction the world is taking. I get tired of intellectuals laughing at religious people. I grow irritated with politicians using religion to get votes. I am incensed at doctors who murder the unborn and at lawyers who defend atrocities. I get sick of pornography passing as art. I become infuriated with governments that oppress their citizens.

But I have to admit that my anger is often misplaced. What should we expect when we leave unbelievers in charge? Instead of being angry at the world, we should be upset with ourselves for letting things get this bad. The world has no solution; God has called *us* to be the solution. He has given us the responsibility of influencing culture for Christ.

But where are the Christian politicians? Where are the Christian playwrights? Where are the believers moving into leadership roles in our colleges and universities? Which followers of Christ will take the high ground in medicine, law, and business? Our generation cries out for guidance and we must provide it.

Where are the leaders? They are here, right now, reading this book. You are the salt of the earth and the light of the world; you are the one to take the world as your project. Christians should seek to advance in government, rather than complaining about political corruption. We should be first in charitable organizations, rather than bemoaning the plight of the poor. We should be at the forefront of ecological projects, rather than laughing at those who celebrate Earth Day. We should be leaders in every good cause. As physical and spiritual descendants of Noah, we have not been called to escape from the world, but to influence it.

How do you handle the opportunity of life that God has given you? Do you ignore his call while the world runs headlong into corruption? You and I must be committed to taking hold of the earthly responsibilities of multiplication and dominion. The world awaits deliverance from the mastery of sin. God has called you and me to set it free. How are you influencing society around you? How are you preparing future generations for effective service in God's world? God's call to Noah to live responsibly as the image of God is our call, too (see Figure 4).

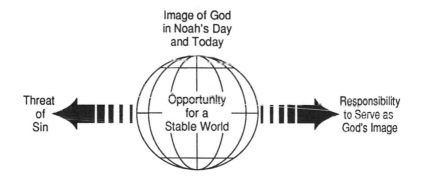

Figure 4. Threat, Opportunity, and Responsibility

CONCLUSION

If we are to turn our lives around, we must remember what we have seen in this chapter. We live in a threatening situation on this earth. Evil constantly seeks to destroy us. God intervened in the days of Noah and gave us an opportunity to rise above the futility of sin. But you and I must take advantage of this opportunity by serving him in this sinful world. When we keep these truths in mind, we will begin to see our lives turn around.

ᔐ   ᔐ   ᔐ

REVIEW QUESTIONS

1. Why must we describe our circumstances as a threatening situation? How did Moses illustrate this truth in Genesis? How is it evident in our day?
2. How did God give his image an opportunity for dignity in the days of Noah? How does this opportunity comfort us?
3. What responsibility did God give to his image in this fallen world? How does Christ confirm our role in this world?

DISCUSSION EXERCISES

1. Why is this chapter entitled "Turning Around"?
2. How has sin attempted to master you in the past? Why did you fail or succeed in mastering sin?
3. What are the most stable things in your life? How do these orderly realities provide you with an opportunity for a meaningful life?
4. Name two ways in which you neglect your earthly responsibilities. What would happen if all Christians did this?

5

REACHING OUR GOAL

"You'd better bring some water," Don warned as we left the house. We were going to hike up a nearby mountain that afternoon and it must have been a hundred degrees Fahrenheit.

"No thanks," I replied. "I won't need any."

It wasn't long, however, before I began to bake in the sun. I realized what a big mistake I had made, but I kept muttering to myself, "I'm not going to ask for water. I'm not going to ask for water." I just couldn't admit I was wrong.

After an hour of walking, we stopped to rest under a small tree. Don pulled out his canteen and took a long, cool drink. "I'm not going to ask. . . . I'm not," I whispered. But when he noticed my red face and parched lips, he offered me some water.

As I grabbed the canteen out of his hand, he smiled and said, "I guess you'll bring along what you need next time."

"You bet I will," I agreed.

In previous chapters we saw that Adam and Eve put the human race under a curse of futility when they rebelled against God. In the days of Noah, God set us on a path toward restoring our dignity by providing a stable world in which we could live for him. Nevertheless, we need to be sure to take along everything we need to reach the end of this road to dignity. What are these necessities? What do we need to be restored as images of God? We will look for answers to these questions in the covenant that God made with Abraham. When God chose Abraham to be his special servant, he showed the Patriarch that he needed power, patience, and perseverance (see Figure 5).

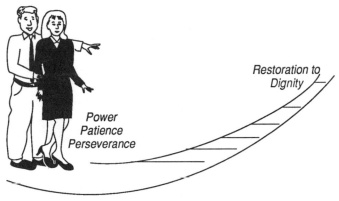

Figure 5. Reaching Our Goal

THE NEED FOR POWER

When NASA scientists launch a rocket, they have a window of opportunity within which they must have lift-off. While this period of time is critical to space flight, much more than opportunity is needed to achieve success. The blinding flames and massive clouds of steam and smoke roaring out of the rocket engines show that space travel also requires tremendous power. In much the same way, we have a window of opportunity as we live in the stable world that God made in Noah's day. Yet, we must also have power to reach the destiny for which God created us.

We read in the fifteenth chapter of Genesis that Abram came to a point in his life where he realized his own need for power. God spoke words to the Patriarch that caused him to examine his life: "Do not be afraid, Abram. I am your shield, your very great reward" (v. 1).

Abram was privileged to have such a marvelous promise from God, but he could not rejoice: "Abram said, 'O Sovereign LORD, what can you give me since I remain childless and the one who will inherit my estate is Eliezer of Damascus?' And Abram said, 'You have given me no children; so a servant in my household will be my heir'" (vv. 2–3).

"Let's get real," Abram thought to himself. "I can't rest assured of great blessings when I don't even have a son." God had promised Abram a son years before, but he still had not fulfilled his word. Abram's hands were tied. He did not have the power to bring a child into the world. What hope could he have?

Later in the same chapter, God offered a second word of assurance to Abram: "I am the LORD, who brought you out of Ur of the Chaldeans to give you this land to take possession of it" (v. 7). In addition to a seed, God promised Abram possession of a land, the land of Canaan.

But this blessing also troubled the Patriarch: "Abram said, 'O Sovereign LORD, how can I know that I will gain possession of it?'" (v. 8). Abram did not understand how Canaan could ever belong to him. "I've got to be honest," he thought. "I do not have the ability to take that land."

We have to be careful here. Abram's concerns were more than the expression of personal desire. They pertained directly to Abram's fundamental task as a human being. He wanted children and a land because he had been created to multiply and have dominion. As far as the Patriarch was concerned, his human dignity was at stake.

More than this, Abram's desire to multiply and have dominion went far beyond his individual life. Abram knew that his seed was critical to the history of the world because God had chosen him to be the spiritual father of all the people who would receive salvation. "All peoples on earth will be blessed through you" (Gen. 12:3), God had told him. As the apostle Paul argued, Christ was the seed of Abram in whom all nations would receive a blessing (Gal. 3:16). Abram desired a line of descendants climaxing in the Christ.

The land that Abram hoped to possess had significance beyond his life, as well. Canaan was a symbolic foretaste of the glorious new heavens and new earth. As the writer of Hebrews put it:

> By faith Abraham, when called to go to a place he would later receive as his inheritance, obeyed and went, even though he did not know where he was going. By faith he made his home in the promised land like a stranger in a foreign country; he lived in tents, as did Isaac and Jacob, who were heirs with him of the same promise. For he was looking forward to the city with foundations, whose architect and builder is God. (Heb. 11:8–10; see also vv. 13–16)

The Patriarch was concerned with his personal dignity, but also with something that affects every one of us. In an ultimate sense, God promised to Abram nothing less than our hope of eternal salvation in Christ, our final restoration as God's images.

Why did Abram struggle? What was the source of his anxiety? Abram wrestled with God's promises because he realized something about himself. He recognized that he could not reach the goals set before him. His wife was barren and he could do nothing about it. Canaanites filled the land of Canaan, and he did not have the strength to dispossess them. God's promises sounded great, but they were far beyond Abram's reach.

Have you ever tried to reach an unattainable goal? It's hard to endure the hardships when you know you'll never succeed. If we have half a chance, most of us will face a challenge. But when the obstacles are insurmountable, we lose all hope. These ordinary experiences give us a glimpse into Abram's feelings. Abram wanted to be all that God had designed him to be; he wanted to multiply and have dominion. But Abram recognized that he simply did not have the power to do it.

Abram's need for power reveals an important truth about each one of us. We too are incapable of reaching our goals as God's images. Acknowledging our impotence is difficult for many of us. On every side the world tells us just the opposite: "Only the strong survive. . . . Success depends on you." We admire the strong; we follow the self-confident. To be sure, we all need a good dose of determination and confidence. Yet, our confidence should not be in ourselves. Successful multiplication and dominion are simply beyond our abilities.

Consider how powerless we are to multiply images of God. Despite advances in reproductive sciences, the miracle of life will always remain beyond our final control. Our limitations also extend to the spiritual dimensions of multiplication. Christian parents raise their children to serve Christ, but they cannot force them into the kingdom. Television, movies, books, schools—even our children's friends—try to draw them away, and we can do little about it. The same is true of multiplying God's image through evangelism and discipleship. We work hard to reach the lost. We try to rescue the wayward, but ultimately we cannot make them remain faithful to Christ. We simply do not have the power.

We are just as incapable of successfully exercising dominion. We plan and perform our jobs the best we can, but success depends on events far beyond our control: international politics, the weather, the stock market. Even the greatest minds don't have the power to manage all the forces that determine success and failure. As a prominent businessman once told me, "I work hard, but I just can't control everything in the world." Dominion over the earth is beyond our power.

In one way or another, all of us wrestle with the problems that plagued Abram. God has spoken wonderful words of promise: "I will grant you dignity in Christ." But we don't have the power to reach this glorious destiny.

What is the answer to this problem? God responded to Abram by revealing the power that would enable him to reach his goals in life. To assure Abram of multiplication, God "took him outside and said, 'Look up at the heavens and count the stars—if indeed you can count them.' Then he said to him, 'So shall your offspring be'" (Gen. 15:5). In effect, God said to Abram, "I have filled the sky with innumerable stars. Surely, I have the power to give you descendants." How did Abram react to these words of assurance? "Abram believed the LORD, and he credited it to him as righteousness" (v. 6). The display of divine strength in the constellations gave Abram confidence that God had the power to give him a child.

The Lord also showed Abram the power that would give him the land of Canaan. This time, however, God commanded him to perform a ceremony: "So the LORD said to him, 'Bring me a heifer, a goat and a ram, each three years old, along with a dove and a young pigeon'" (Gen. 15:9). The Patriarch gathered the animals, took out his knife, and cut all but the birds in half. After tearing the carcasses, he laid them on opposite sides of a pathway (v. 10).

The Israelites who first heard Moses tell this story understood these bizarre actions. God ordered Abram to perform a type of ancient ceremony mentioned elsewhere in the Bible (1 Sam. 17:44, 46; Jer. 34:18–20). In these ceremonies, animals were slaughtered, carnage was laid on either side of a path, and the parties of a covenant passed between the two rows. As they walked among the torn flesh, the parties took a serious vow: "If we break our agreement, may we be torn apart like these animals."

Little children do something similar today. When they want their friends to trust their word, they call curses on themselves: "Cross my heart; hope to die; stick a needle in my eye!" In effect they say, "If I break my word, here's a target over my heart; you may kill me. You also have permission to stick a needle in my eye." Or, as we sometimes say, "If I'm lyin', I'm dyin'."

In response to Abram's request, God ordered a ceremony that normally required both parties to swear curses on themselves. It's no wonder that Abram had a terrible nightmare as he fell asleep that night (Gen. 15:12). He must have been frightened out of his mind. "I asked God to assure me that I'd get the land. Now look what I've done," he must have thought to himself. "God is going to make *me* walk between the animals and swear to my own destruction that *I* will take the land!"

But God surprised Abram during the night: "When the sun had set and darkness had fallen, a smoking firepot with a blazing torch appeared and passed between the pieces" (Gen. 15:17). Every Israelite hearing this story knew what this smoke and fire represented. God had appeared on Mount Sinai and led Israel through the wilderness as a pillar of cloud and fire (Ex. 13:21). The smoke and fire that passed between the pieces that night was a theophany, an appearance of the same God who went before Israel toward the Promised Land.

By passing between the rows of carnage, God swore a curse on himself. He said, "If I do not keep my promise to you, Abram, may I be torn to pieces even as these animals have been torn." On threat of his own destruction, God promised that *his* power would give Abram dominion over the Promised Land.

Abram learned an essential lesson that day. To reach his destiny as God's image, he had to take his eyes off of his own impotence and trust completely in divine power. Only God had the ability to multiply his seed and give him dominion.

As God's redeemed images today, we yearn to fill the world with God's servants and to rule victoriously over the earth. But where do we look for the power to succeed in these tasks? How can we find assurance that we will reach such a glorious goal? We must learn with Abram that we can succeed, not by our own efforts, but only by faith in God's power.

83

Abram discovered his source of power when he counted the stars and saw the theophany of smoke and fire. We have seen even more than he did. God became flesh, tabernacled among us, and passed before us in the Incarnation. Jesus came and secured our salvation, so that God could be "just and the one who justifies" (Rom. 3:26). Our dignity is restored solely by God's power in Christ. We find the strength we need only in his finished work.

We all know the doctrine of salvation by grace through faith. "For it is by grace you have been saved, through faith," we repeat to ourselves, "and this not from yourselves" (Eph. 2:8). We know that God alone raises us out of the mire of sin. On a theoretical level, we have little problem with what Abram learned.

But more often than not, we have a hard time translating this belief into daily practice. In theory we say, "Saved by grace," but in practice we declare, "Saved by my own power." Take a hard look at yourself. Where do you put your hope for dignity? On whom do you depend to be successful as the image of God?

Think about your efforts to multiply God's image by raising your children. The measure of your reliance on God becomes evident when you see how little you go to God in prayer about your children. How much do you pray for your sons and daughters? How much do you seek the help of the only One who can save them? Most Christian parents work diligently to raise their children in the ways of Christ. They discipline them, pay large sums of money for Christian education, and take them to church every Sunday. These activities are important, but they are useless unless God empowers them to benefit our children. Our daily practices reveal that we rely much more on our own strength than on God's power to mold our children in the likeness of God.

The same is true in all of our other tasks in life. What priorities do we exhibit in our jobs? We plan, work, and struggle; then we plan, work, and struggle some more. Conscious reliance on God hardly figures into our lifestyles. We turn to him only when all else fails. Hard work is vital, but we demonstrate faithful trust in God only as we bathe our efforts in devotion and prayer.

I remember a time when my wife and I were about to go on a trip. Our car had been running poorly for several weeks, but I thought I would save a few dollars and work on it myself. I was confident that I had fixed the problem, but my wife wasn't so sure. "We'll never make it," she said as we packed the car. "You should have taken it to someone who could get the job done."

To my chagrin, her words proved to be true. The car broke down before we had gone ten miles. Fortunately, we had a friend who was a professional mechanic, and he repaired the car in just a few minutes. As we drove out of town later that day, both my wife and I were confident that we would reach our destination. Unlike before, the car had been fixed by someone who had the ability to do the job.

Why is it so important to remember that God has the power to raise us to dignity? What is the benefit? He can do the job! In Genesis 15 we see how Abram gained confidence about his future. He stopped asking questions and looking for assurances. Once he understood that God would use his own power to lift him up, Abram believed God and moved forward with confidence. "Now I know where to put my trust," Abram realized. "I can get on with reaching my destiny."

The same is true for us as we yearn for success as God's images. If we trust in ourselves to reach the goal, we will surely be disappointed. But as we trust in him from day to day, we can have confidence that we will reach our goal as images of God.

THE NEED FOR PATIENCE

A few years ago, some friends invited my family for lunch. "Just come over and relax," they said. "We'll take care of everything." It sounded great; we were exhausted from a week of hard work. But when we arrived at our friends' house, it soon became apparent that they had not planned on us coming. We waited while they worked in the kitchen. Then we waited some more. More than two hours passed before we heard the call to lunch. I was famished as I sat down. But I remember thinking to myself, "I guess you have to be ready to wait, if someone else is doing all the work."

Abram faced a similar situation in his life. He was not waiting for someone to cook him a meal—he was waiting for God to give him a son. In Genesis 15, God invited Abram to trust divine power for his dignity. "I'll do it for you," God assured him. Abram liked that idea; it was comforting to know that he did not have to secure his dignity through his own ingenuity. Nevertheless, Abram failed to see that he would have to be patient if God was going to do all the work.

Genesis 16 is a story of Abram's failure to exercise patience. Abram and Sarai determined to have Hagar, Sarai's handmaiden, serve as a surrogate mother: "Now Sarai, Abram's wife, had borne him no children. But she had an Egyptian maidservant named Hagar; so she said to Abram, 'The LORD has kept me from having children. Go, sleep with my maidservant; perhaps I can build a family through her'" (vv. 1–2). As the chapter tells us, Abram carried through with the plan. Hagar conceived and gave birth to Abram's first child, Ishmael.

What led Abram to follow this course of action? In a word, the problem was impatience. Abram and Sarai liked the idea that God would give them a son, but they had already been waiting for a number of years. God did not act according to their timing; he was too slow for them. Consequently, Abram and Sarai chose their own way to secure their dignity.

We face the same problem with impatience today. We are glad that we do not have to merit our salvation. Who doesn't rejoice to know that our success as God's image is entirely a gift of his grace? Nevertheless, if we want to rely on the power of God, we must be ready to wait patiently on him. We have to trust him to grant us dignity as he sees fit.

We live in a culture of instant results. We develop a photograph in a few seconds, microwave a meal in a matter of minutes, and travel from one side of the world to the other in less than a day. We are so used to instant results that we grow impatient with anything that takes time. "How much longer will that waiter take?" we complain in the restaurant. "Hurry up!" we shout at the car in front of us. "I've got a million things to do!"

The desire for instant results flows into our spiritual lives as well. We know from Scripture that God has promised us rich blessings in his Son. But we are impatient for those blessings; we want them now. We have become "heirs of God and coheirs with Christ" (Rom. 8:17), but we want to experience the full benefits of this status immediately.

We must face the reality that God does not want to give us all of our blessings in Christ at once. In his unsearchable wisdom, God restores his people over a long period of time. Before Christ returns in glory, the only portion of our inheritance that God guarantees is the gift of the Holy Spirit. The Spirit is the "deposit guaranteeing our inheritance" (Eph. 1:14). To be sure, we often receive many extra benefits beyond the foretaste of the Spirit—health, money, honor—but God grants these bits and pieces of our inheritance in Christ only as he sees fit. He gives some blessings to one person and other blessings to another. He remedies some aspects of our ignobility and leaves others until later.

God's plan sounds fine in the abstract, but when we face particular needs in our lives, his timing does not suit us any better than it did Abram. The Patriarch must have sat and wondered, "If I'm God's special servant, why don't I have a son when others have so many children?" Haven't we all felt the same way? We see the blessings God gives to others and jealousy overwhelms us. "Look at that guy," we say. "Why don't I have a job that pays as much as his?" "I only wish my children were as good as theirs," we lament.

All of us wrestle with such thoughts from time to time. Look at yourself. What are the areas of life in which you lack the honor that you deserve as God's child—your bank account, your health, your job, your family life? While it is difficult not to compare yourself with others, it is foolish to do so. As time inevitably proves, God does not cheat his children. He simply gives them the blessings of dignity according to his own schedule. As faithful servants, we must wait for God to grant his gifts as he sees fit. Patience is essential for reaching the goal of dignity.

What happens to those who become impatient? To understand the dangers, we need to remember three things about Abram's failure. First, Abram did not pursue the lusts of the flesh. He was not going after selfish gain. Abram was simply trying to fulfill a legitimate expectation as God's redeemed image. The Patriarch was made for the purpose of multiplying God's servants. That's all he wanted. Abram's problem was not that he desired a son; rather, it was that he sought to get one by the wrong means.

We face the same dangers in our own lives. We have legitimate expectations, but we become impatient. As a result, we look for substitutes and go after dignity in ways that are inappropriate. Our desires may be correct, but our plans may be wrong.

Second, Abram and Sarai's actions were respectable but immoral. They turned away from the promises of God, but their actions were quite acceptable by the standards of their society. Abram did not pursue his goal by committing flagrant, horrible crimes that everyone hated. Instead, he sought his dignity down a path that everyone around him followed.

Isn't this just like you and me? Few of us rob banks to gain the honor of riches. We don't get ahead in business by murdering our competitors. We don't fulfill our desire to multiply by kidnapping someone else's children. Most Christians are not seriously tempted to do such things. Instead, we turn to culturally respectable sins, just as Abram did.

What kinds of sins do we commit? We gossip, lie, and cheat. We tighten the reins on our children and provoke them to bitterness. We break the Sabbath to get ahead at work. We hold back our tithes to buy a new car. We pursue these substitutes for God-given dignity. "It's no big deal," we say. "Everybody does it." We commit respectable sins, knowing that no one will call our hand.

Third, Abram's plan seemed to succeed at first, but in the end it failed. His impatience led him to seek a son "according to the flesh" (Gal. 4:23, NASB). God had promised that Abram's multiplication would come through a miracle child, but the Patriarch sought a substitute. Everything seemed great for a while, but Abram's substitute for God's blessing soon began to crumble before his eyes. Jealousy consumed Sarai and she drove Hagar away (Gen. 16:6). God delivered Hagar and her son from this trouble (v. 7) and promised to bless Ishmael (v. 10). Yet, the substitute in whom Abram put his hope would turn out to be trouble for the people of God throughout history: "He will be a wild donkey of a man; his hand will be against everyone and everyone's hand against him, and he will live in hostility toward all his brothers" (v. 12). Abram's impatience drew him into a path that could never lead to blessing. It only brought him trouble.

This is why we must be so careful not to follow our own ways to dignity. The substitutes we pursue out of impatience sometimes give the impression of success. The businessman who cheats often gets ahead of others. Lies may keep us out of trouble for a while. We become involved in these substitutes for faith in God because they appear to benefit us. Sooner or later, however, our actions will turn against us. Impatience will not lead to dignity; eventually it will bring us to further ignobility.

Abram's failure to wait for God speaks directly to you and me. We must rely on God to give us our dignity, but this reliance entails patience. To reach our goal of being restored as the image of God, we must wait for God to give us gifts of dignity according to his design. However long it takes, we must demonstrate our trust in his grace by waiting for him.

THE NEED FOR PERSEVERANCE

A few years ago, I walked into our kitchen and saw my four-year-old daughter with a butcher's knife. She was holding a block of cheese in one hand and the knife in the other. Immediately I cried, "Put that knife down! You're going to cut yourself!"

"No I'm not," she replied confidently. "The knife is slicing the cheese, not my hand."

Of course, I didn't try to convince her; I just grabbed the knife and took it away. I knew something about knives that she had not yet learned. Knives cut in more ways than one. The same blade that slices food can cut the hand that holds it. The same instrument that gives life can take life.

As we have seen, God used a knife in Genesis 15 to assure Abram that he would receive great blessings in the future. God passed under the knife, guaranteeing that he would use his own power to raise Abram to greater dignity. But now we must turn to Genesis 17, where God tells Abram to bring the knife out again. This time, however, God does not assure Abram. He uses the knife to warn the Patriarch that he must persevere.

Genesis 17 begins with God confronting Abram for his impatience in Genesis 16: "When Abram was ninety-nine years old, the LORD appeared to him and said, 'I am God Almighty; walk before me and be blameless. I will confirm my covenant between me and you and will greatly increase your numbers'" (vv. 1–2). The Lord told Abram that he had to get his life in order. Instead of following his own way, as he had with Hagar, Abram had to walk blamelessly before God. The Patriarch recognized the gravity of his sin and lowered himself to the ground in repentance (v. 3). He realized anew that fidelity to God was required of all who want to be restored to dignity.

To deal with Abram's waywardness, God explained the two sides of his covenant relationship with him. He spoke first of divine promise, and then he addressed Abram's human responsibility. Genesis 17:4–8 describes what Abram could expect from God. "As for me," he began (v. 4), "this is my covenant with you." God pledged to do great things for Abram. He promised to make Abram's descendants exceedingly numerous (vv. 4–7) and to give them the land of Canaan (v. 8). Accordingly, he renamed him Abraham, which means "father of many (nations)" (v. 5).

In verse 9, however, a major shift occurs. Instead of speaking of what he will do for Abraham, God turns to Abraham's responsibility: "As for you, you must keep my covenant, you and your descendants after you for the generations to come." God had given great promises to Abraham; now he states explicitly that Abraham and his descendants have a responsibility. They must "keep my covenant" (v. 9). They must remain faithful to God in order to receive the promised blessings.

Doesn't this passage contradict the promises given in Genesis 15? Didn't God tell Abraham that reaching the goal of restoration depended entirely on divine grace? Is God adding a new requirement here, changing the rules in the middle of the game?

No. God was not revising his relationship with Abraham. He simply brought to the foreground a truth that had faded from Abraham's memory. Throughout Abraham's life, God had made it clear that fidelity was required. Even the initial call of the Patriarch pointed to the need for appropriate human response: "The LORD had said to Abram, 'Leave your country, your people and your father's household and go to the land I will show you. I will make you into a great nation and I will bless you'" (Gen. 12:1–2).

91

Abraham would be blessed only if he left his country and followed God to the Land of Promise.

Unfortunately, Abraham forgot that God required obedience. He took the gracious promises of Genesis 15 as a license to do what he pleased. Now, however, God reminded him that those who want to receive the promises of grace must remain loyal.

Moses first recorded the events of Genesis 17 to warn his readers against turning away from God. The Israelites following Moses were a fickle group. They followed him out of Egypt, only to turn against God time and time again; they took the grace of God as an opportunity to sin. But the record of God's word to Abraham reminded the Israelites of their responsibility. To be the covenant people, they had to walk in fidelity to their covenant vows.

The apostle Paul dealt with the same issue in the Book of Romans. In chapters 4 and 5 he established that salvation is by grace alone. We are redeemed by the mercies of God, not by human effort. Our good works do not merit salvation. Yet, after emphasizing God's grace, the apostle added a crucial reminder: "What shall we say, then? Shall we go on sinning so that grace may increase? By no means! We died to sin; how can we live in it any longer?" (Rom. 6:1–2).

God's grace is never intended to encourage us to go our own way. We are set free from sin in order to live in gratitude and obedience. Paul summed up this relationship between grace and works in a well-known passage in Ephesians: "For it is by grace you have been saved, through faith—and this not from yourselves, it is the gift of God—not by works, so that no one can boast" (Eph. 2:8–9). Just as God told Abraham about his grace in Genesis 15, so Paul affirmed in Ephesians 2:8–9 that the restoration of God's image is entirely the result of grace. Yet, notice the focus of the verse that follows: "For we are God's workmanship, created in Christ Jesus to do good works, which God prepared in advance for us to do" (v. 10).

Why does God show us grace? What should we do in

response to his kindness? We must walk before God in the good works that he foreordained for us to do.

Many things in life come in pairs. Some pairs are easy to keep together. Trousers, for instance, don't normally come apart. It's unusual to lose one lens from your glasses. Other pairs, however, are hard to keep together. I have at least four different right-hand gloves in my drawer at home. I also have lots of socks that don't have a match. Gloves and socks come in pairs, but they are hard to keep together.

In Genesis 15 and 17 we have a pair of concepts that most Christians find hard to keep together. These chapters tell us the importance of faith and fidelity, but we tend to forget one or the other. There are many people in the church who think they can earn their own salvation. "Just be good enough and you'll get into heaven," they imagine. But Genesis 15 opposes this idea. We cannot be restored by our own power. The only way is to rely on the grace of God in Christ.

But there are others in the church who believe they can live in rebellion against God and still be saved from his judgment. "It doesn't matter how you live," they advise. "Just believe." Genesis 17 opposes this error. Saving faith will always be accompanied by a life of good works.

To demonstrate how serious this matter was for Abraham, God ordered him to bring his knife out again. It was time to do some more cutting: "This is my covenant with you and your descendants after you, the covenant you are to keep: Every male among you shall be circumcised. You are to undergo circumcision, and it will be the sign of the covenant between me and you" (Gen. 17:10–11).

What did the cutting ritual of circumcision depict? It set apart Abraham and his children as participants in God's covenant, but it also symbolized human responsibility in the covenant. In Genesis 15, God placed himself under the knife. "May I be cut to pieces if I break my pledge," God swore to Abram. In Genesis 17, God commanded Abraham and his descendants to go under the knife. The rite of circumcision symbolized their commitment to loyalty and fidelity. "May we be cut off as our foreskin is cut off, if we break our pledge of fidelity to God," they vowed.

Abraham's knife portrayed in a vivid fashion what happens to those who flagrantly violate their covenant relationship. It warned Abraham and his seed that they would not escape the wrath of God if they spurned the way of faithful living. Instead of reaching the goal of restoration, apostates will suffer God's judgment.

Two clarifications should be added. First, Abraham's circumcision does not imply that we can lose our salvation. Everyone who comes to Christ with genuine faith is secure in him. It is impossible to lose the gift of salvation. Jesus made this clear: "All that the Father gives me will come to me, and whoever comes to me I will never drive away. . . . And this is the will of him who sent me, that I shall lose none of all that he has given me, but raise them up at the last day" (John 6:37, 39).

For this reason, the threat symbolized in circumcision is not for true believers who temporarily lapse into sin. It is for those who outwardly profess Christ without possessing him. Their apostasy proves the true condition of their heart. Those who continue in a lifestyle contrary to Christ have never exercised saving faith. As John puts it, "They went out from us, but they did not really belong to us. For if they had belonged to us, they would have remained with us; but their going showed that none of them belonged to us" (1 John 2:19). Those who utterly fall away from Christ never truly belonged to him. If they had, they would have demonstrated their salvation by remaining faithful.

Second, we must understand that circumcision did not imply that God was waiting for any excuse to cut off Abraham from his blessings. The Scriptures are clear that God is patient and long-suffering. He is "gracious and compassionate, slow to anger and abounding in love, and he relents from sending calamity" (Joel 2:13). God is very slow to become angry with his people. He loves to show mercy and forbearance toward us when we sin.

Nevertheless, Scripture severely warns those who turn away from Christ and continue unrepentant. The threat of God's judgment, both now and in eternity, stands over them. Flagrant, unrelenting apostasy will result in the curse of the covenant. As Paul warned the Galatians: "Do not be deceived: God cannot be mocked. A man reaps what he sows. The one who sows to please his sinful nature, from that nature will reap destruction; the one who sows to please the Spirit, from the Spirit will reap eternal life. Let us not become weary in doing good, for at the proper time we will reap a harvest if we do not give up" (Gal. 6:7–9).

God's word to Abraham is a warning to each one of us. We are all prone to wander from time to time. The path toward restoration as God's image is narrow and treacherous. Temptations come our way and we stumble, just like Abraham. Forgiveness is available to those who confess their sins (1 John 1:9), but we must not take the availability of forgiveness for granted. Pursuing the pleasures of possessions, prestige, or any other sinful substitute for God's promises in Christ is a dangerous path to follow. As the writer of Hebrews said, "Without holiness no one will see the Lord" (Heb. 12:14). We cannot have Jesus as Savior unless we also have him as Lord. As Abraham learned, believers must not only trust God for their salvation, but also persevere in their fidelity to him.

How are you tempted to take God's grace as permission to sin? Hear the word of the Lord to Abraham. To reach our goal of being restored to dignity, we must walk before him and be blameless.

CONCLUSION

In this chapter we have examined three things that are necessary for reaching our dignity as the image of God. We must have faith in God's power to take us there, exercise patience as we wait for God's timing, and faithfully persevere throughout our lives. Only as we remember what God revealed to Abraham will we be able to reach the goal of fully restoring our dignity as the image of God.

ða   ða   ða

REVIEW QUESTIONS

1. With what two issues did Abram wrestle in Genesis 15? How does this chapter focus on our need to rely on the power of God?
2. What failure occurred in Genesis 16? How does this story reveal Abram's impatience? What dangers lie ahead of those who refuse to wait for God's timing?
3. What did Abraham learn through the rite of circumcision in Genesis 17? Is it possible for true believers to lose their salvation in Christ? If not, how can we speak of the necessity of perseverance?

DISCUSSION EXERCISES

1. Why is this chapter entitled "Reaching Our Goal"?
2. Name three tasks you are sure you can perform. Now think again. What factors beyond your control could make these tasks impossible? How do these realities illustrate your need for God's power to give you dignity?
3. How have you seen impatience with God's timing in the church? Have the results been positive or negative? Why?
4. What kinds of experiences have you seen lead people away from Christ? How have you wrestled with perseverance in the faith?

6

FIGHTING TO WIN

The United States learned some difficult lessons from the Vietnam War. Controversies still rage over many aspects of the conflict. Where did we go wrong? As I have talked with men and women who fought in Vietnam, one point of view has come up again and again. "If you're going to fight," one soldier told me, "you've got to fight to win." That's one opinion all of us can affirm. If we have to fight in a war, we'd better fight to win.

As we continue to explore God's plan for his image, we come to a time when he called his people to enter a war. We have already seen God's rich blessings in the days of Noah and Abraham. God provided us with the opportunity to rise out of sin's corruption, and he revealed the power, patience, and perseverance necessary for regaining the dignity that we corrupted in the Fall. In this chapter we will move to the next milestone in biblical history: the ministry of Moses. As we will see, God used Moses to lead his people another step closer to full restoration as images of God. He called them to a war they had to fight to win.

THE REALITY OF WAR

Moses is perhaps the most important human figure in the Old Testament. He delivered the tribes of Israel from bondage in Egypt, led them through the wilderness, and brought them to the border of the Promised Land. Why did God have Moses do these things? Joshua discovered that the purpose of Moses' ministry was to bring God's people face-to-face with the reality of war.

God came to Joshua after Moses died and informed him that it was time to go into Canaan. "Get ready to cross the Jordan River into the land" (Josh. 1:2), God declared. Then he added, "No one will be able to stand up against you" (v. 5).

To grasp the significance of Joshua's call to war, we must remember what was in store for Israel in the land of Canaan. Canaan would be a place of unimaginable blessing. Once settled there, God's people would multiply beyond measure, filling the land from end to end with images of God (Deut. 28:5, 11). Israel would also exercise dominion over the earth as never before. Futility in work would diminish; the earth would yield fruit with minimal labor (Deut. 28:12). Put simply, God designed Canaan to be a place of tremendous dignity for his redeemed images. By fighting for Canaan, Israel would get a taste of the honor for which God had originally designed the human race. God came to Joshua with solemn instructions. "You must fight," he said, "for the honor of living in the Promised Land."

Every believer stands where Joshua stood that day, because God has called us to fight for our dignity. Christ has set us free from sin, just as Moses set Israel free from slavery. We move toward the glory of the new heavens and the new earth, just as Israel moved toward the land of Canaan. But we too must go to war, just as Israel went to war. Dignity as God's image does not come to us on a silver platter; like Joshua, we must fight for it.

Although the parallels between our circumstances and Israel's situation are profound, we have to be careful to understand the differences as well. Christ has not left us with the legacy of a physical holy war. Until he returns in glory, our war is a spiritual battle. As Paul put it, "Our struggle is not against flesh and blood, but against the rulers, against the authorities, against the powers of this dark world and against the spiritual forces of evil in the heavenly realms" (Eph. 6:12).

We do not take on the armies of the nations; rather, we do battle with spiritual forces. We fight against falsehoods and lies, using the weapons supplied by the Holy Spirit:

> For though we live in the world, we do not wage war as the world does. The weapons we fight with are not the weapons of the world. On the contrary, they have divine power to demolish strongholds. We demolish arguments and every pretension that sets itself up against the knowledge of God, and we take captive every thought to make it obedient to Christ. (2 Cor. 10:3–5)

God has called every Christian to this battle for dignity. He has offered us great promises, but his promises come only to those who are ready to fight and win.

A young man once came up to me after an evangelistic meeting. "I'm so glad you told us the truth," he said with a smile.

"What do you mean?" I asked.

"When I became a Christian," he explained, "the preacher told me my life would be easy. He said Jesus would take away all my troubles. I would never have to struggle again."

"It's just not true, is it?" I replied.

"That's for sure!" he shouted. "When I became a Christian, I felt like I was thrown into the middle of a nuclear war!"

If you follow Christ, you are in a war. Your success in multiplying and exercising dominion—your growth in dignity as God's image—will not come easily. These blessings are gained only through spiritual warfare. In our battles, we seek the lost for Christ. We struggle with recurring sins. We face illness and death. We fight battles for the truth. We face all kinds of conflicts.

Can you imagine how Joshua must have felt when he contemplated the reality of war? Possessing Canaan was a glorious destiny, but the prospect of battle must have been daunting. As Joshua considered the massive fortifications and strong armies ahead of him, he must have had second thoughts. "How can I fulfill this call? I know I must fight, but it won't be easy."

We know that these concerns weighed heavily on the young warrior's heart, because of God's word to him in Joshua 1:6–9. In this passage God addressed Joshua's fear by repeating the same injunction three times: "Be strong and courageous. . . . Be strong and very courageous. . . . Be strong and courageous."

As we will see, however, God did more than simply command Joshua to keep a stiff upper lip. He told Joshua three specific ways in which he could build up his strength and courage. Joshua had to hold firmly to God's purpose, guidance, and presence. Joshua could fight valiantly by remembering these things. As we examine God's instructions to Joshua, we will learn how to have strength and courage in the battles ahead of us (see Figure 6).

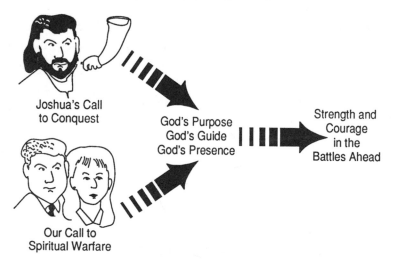

Figure 6. Our Call to War

GOD'S PURPOSE

I remember the first time some friends and I went behind the Iron Curtain on an evangelistic mission. Many worries distracted us. What would happen if our literature was discovered? Would they put us in jail? Would we be able to return home? As you can imagine, these worries brought all kinds of doubts and confusion. How did we combat this discouragement? The strategy was simple. The leaders of our group kept reminding us of our purpose. "We are not here to see the country. We are not here to think about ourselves. We are here to tell people about Christ," they kept saying. When we fixed our minds on that specific goal, our fear dissipated. We found courage to move ahead by keeping our purpose before us.

In much the same way, God encouraged Joshua by telling him to keep his heart fixed on his specific purpose: "Be strong and courageous, because you will lead these people to inherit the land I swore to their forefathers to give them" (Josh. 1:6). In effect, the Lord told Joshua, "I have designed you for the specific task of leading my people into Canaan. If you set your thoughts on this goal, then you will be strong and courageous throughout the struggles ahead." With God's purpose for his life in mind, Joshua could ignore the many distractions around him and move ahead with confidence.

God's encouragement to Joshua applies to us as we face our spiritual warfare. God has not called us to be generals in an army, but he has given each of us specific purposes in our spiritual war. We too can have strength and courage as we focus our hearts on these goals.

As I have traveled around the country, I have seen basically two kinds of churches. On the one hand, many churches have only a vague idea of their goals. "We are here to serve the Lord," the church leaders say. But that's about as specific as they get. Invariably, these churches are filled with people who are tired and discouraged. They are not ex-

101

cited about their faith; they have little spiritual energy. The cares of life weigh them down, and they are so distracted that they can do no more than maintain the status quo.

On the other hand, I have visited a number of churches that have clearly defined purposes. They know what ministries God expects them to perform. They recognize how he wants their church to serve in their particular community. Interestingly enough, most of these churches are filled with enthusiasm. Troubles may come, but the people move forward because their eyes are fixed on their goals. Trials and hardships are pushed aside as these churches press toward their specific goals.

The same is true of individual believers. If we hope to have courage in the battles that lie ahead of us, we must devote ourselves to the purposes for which God put us in this world. One general purpose extends to all: to multiply God's images and have dominion over the earth. But we must go further and lay hold of the specific role each of us has within this general purpose.

For some of us, gaining a specific purpose in life involves making radical changes in lifestyle. Many Christians have never considered the possibility that God might want them to do something extraordinary. They simply do whatever comes their way. Many university students have no sense of direction. Countless middle-aged adults feel stuck in jobs they hate. Retirees confess a lack of direction in life. If this is your lot, you should ponder the possibility of making a significant change. Some of us should leave the comforts to which we have grown accustomed and press toward a radically new direction in life. Then we will find strength and courage to fight for dignity.

I have a friend who took early retirement as a corporate executive in order to teach the children of foreign missionaries. One summer I had the opportunity to visit the city where he lived. When I saw how hard he was working, I joked a bit with him. "I thought you were retired," I remarked.

He wiped the sweat off his face and smiled. "I am retired," he said, "but I'm not dead!"

To tell you the truth, I had never seen him so alive. He had made a radical change in his life. He had new purpose and specific direction. As a result, he was overflowing with zeal for Christ.

From time to time, all of us need to open ourselves up to the possibility of a radical call from God. When was the last time you honestly considered whether God wanted you to make a drastic change? Have you pondered a ministry to the poor, the sick, or prisoners? What about foreign missions? These jobs take deep commitment, but God calls many of us to these kinds of tasks.

Needless to say, God does not want all of us to leave our current callings for a new course in life. Some of us are right where the Lord wants us to be. We simply need renewed purpose rather than a new job.

Several years ago, a businessman came to me with a confession. "For years I thought I was wasting my life in the corporate world. But now I love what I'm doing."

"Did you switch jobs?" I asked.

"No," he responded, "I got down on my knees and asked God to show me what he wanted me to do. I was ready to do anything, but I soon discovered that God had me right where I belonged."

"So what changed?"

"Now I do my job for Christ—and it's great!"

It is easy to fall into the rut of simply doing what we've always done and never asking why we devote ourselves to a calling. To find strength and courage as Joshua did, we must be clear about the purposes that undergird our activities. Why do you devote yourself to the tasks in your life? Do you have a conscious sense of responsibility to God? Do you serve him in your job? To be courageous in the face of struggles, all of us must know that God has called us to our specific tasks and fulfill them for him.

Joshua had to keep his heart fixed on God's purpose.

This was the only way he could move toward victory in Canaan. To face our spiritual warfare with strength and courage, we must also devote ourselves to the purposes for which God has called us.

GOD'S RELIABLE GUIDE

My family and I recently visited Melbourne, Australia, for the first time. Some Aussie friends loaned us their map of the metropolitan area. This was no ordinary map that you slip into your coat pocket—it was a 300-page book. Everywhere we went, people could tell we were tourists because we carried that huge map. Their smirks made us feel uncomfortable at times, but we kept flipping through the pages. Why didn't we just put the map away? The answer is simple. That map would keep us from getting lost. Although it was embarrassing, we were not about to give up our only reliable guide.

As God prepared Joshua for war, he reminded him of his need for a reliable guide: "Be strong and very courageous. Be careful to obey all the law my servant Moses gave you" (Josh. 1:7). How could the leader of Israel's holy army face the battles ahead? How could he have confidence about the decisions he had to make? God told Joshua, "The Law of Moses is your guide. You can have courage if you follow it."

As we enter our spiritual battles, we also need sure direction. Just as God's map for Joshua was the Law of Moses, our map is the entire Bible. Just like Joshua, we must depend on God's revelation in Scripture as we move into our warfare.

To stress the importance of following the Law of Moses, God made a remarkable promise to Joshua. He guaranteed great success if Joshua obeyed the law: "Do not turn from it to the right or to the left, that you may be successful wherever you go. . . . Be careful to do everything written in it. Then you will be prosperous and successful" (Josh. 1:7–8). God explained that obedience to his directions insured success in battle and prosperity in the land of Canaan. The Law of Moses would lead God's people toward tremendous blessings.

God's promise of success and prosperity applies to us today, but we must be careful to understand it properly. Just the other day I heard a television preacher read this passage. He then promised his listeners health and wealth if they observed God's Word and sent money to his ministry. "Just believe the Bible," he exhorted, "and God will take away your diseases and make you rich!"

How tragic. When we read this passage, we must remember the kind of warfare in which we are engaged. We are not fighting a physical war, as Joshua did. Therefore, our successes are not physical, either. God's word to Joshua does not guarantee physical blessings to us at the present time. To be sure, when Christ returns we will inherit all the riches of the earth. But prior to his return, God's promise to Joshua assures us of spiritual, not physical, success and prosperity. If we follow God's Word, we will have success in our struggles with sin in the present and heap up heavenly treasures for the future.

This positive outlook on God's Word is just the opposite of what most people think today. We do not look at the commands of Scripture as beneficial; we consider them restrictive. The Bible is like a straitjacket, a ball and chain that keeps us from enjoying the good things of life. "If only we could be free from the rules of religion," we say to ourselves, "then we could have all kinds of fun."

I remember an episode of a popular television show that illustrated how many people look at God's law. During a chapel service, the army chaplain was reading the Ten Commandments while people yawned, napped, and flipped through magazines, but his words soon got everyone's attention. "Thou shalt not kill," he read. "Thou *shalt* commit adultery." The printers had accidentally deleted "not."

105

When the soldiers heard the revision of the seventh commandment, they all began to shout and dance with glee. "Now we can do what we have wanted to do all along," they thought to themselves. "Now we are really free!"

Most people look at the instructions of the Bible in just that way. They view God's Word as if it were designed to oppress and destroy human life. God gave us sexual desires, but then insisted, "Thou shalt not commit adultery." He made us long for riches, but then commanded, "Thou shalt not steal." What a dirty trick!

Unfortunately, negative outlooks on God's law are not found only outside the church. They are also found among the people of God. A number of denominations and Christian organizations look down on the moral law of God. "We live in the New Testament age," they say. "We don't live with the shackles of rules anymore; we live in the freedom of the Spirit."

As popular as these outlooks may be, they are just the opposite of what God said to Joshua. The principles contained in the Law of Moses enrich life. As Paul put it, "So then, the law is holy, and the commandment is holy, righteous and good" (Rom. 7:12). The law was designed to be a blessing, not a curse: "If you fully obey the LORD your God and carefully follow all his commands I give you today, the LORD your God will set you high above all the nations on earth. All these blessings will come upon you and accompany you if you obey the LORD your God" (Deut. 28:1–2).

However, the Scriptures do teach that God's law can become a curse in the hands of sinful people. If we try to earn our salvation by obeying the law, we find ourselves bound to the futility of legalism. The guidelines of Scripture bring only death to those who try to merit God's favor through compliance with the law.

Nevertheless, once our hearts are transformed by the saving power of Christ, we gain new attitudes toward God's law. We no longer try to earn our way to heaven; we receive our eternal destiny as a free gift. But with new hearts empowered by the Holy Spirit, we delight in the law and find blessings in it.

I know a student who came to the United States a few years ago. As a child in his native country, he shared a one-room apartment with his parents and five brothers and sisters. He had absolutely no privacy; his bedroom amounted to a corner where he spread his pallet every evening. When this young man came to college in the States, he received his own private dormitory room. His new room was little more than a big closet, but by comparison with his home it was huge. "I couldn't believe it," he told me. "I couldn't believe that the whole room was for me!" Once he settled down and began to study, his small quarters became his castle. It made it possible for him to have a fruitful and productive life.

Ironically, just a few miles away a number of young men were living in quarters about the same size as my friend's dormitory room. They spent many hours in their rooms as well, but these men did not see their living space as castles. They were inmates in the state penitentiary. For them the same amount of space was a restrictive prison, not the opportunity for a fruitful life.

We can look at the law of God in both of these ways. If our hearts are hardened by sin, we will see God's rules as confining prison cells. But if our hearts have been renewed by God's grace, we will view the regulations of Scripture as wonderful guides to dignity.

All of us need to step back and examine our attitudes toward Scripture. You may believe that the Bible is God's Word; you may be committed to obeying God's commands. But what is your attitude toward the principles of Scripture? Are they heavy burdens? Or do you realize that they are for your benefit?

Consider the Ten Commandments. Why did God give these laws? We know that he ordained them to bring glory to himself. This is the ultimate end for which all things are designed. "For from him and through him and to him are all things. To him be the glory forever! Amen" (Rom. 11:36).

Even so, the glorification of God is only one reason for these laws. God's word to Joshua tells us that the commandments also benefit us as the image of God.

Why did God command, "You shall have no other gods before me" (Ex. 20:3)? This principle obviously brings honor to God, but it also helps us. People today put all kinds of gods before the Lord: money, intellectual pursuits, romantic relationships, even nationalism. One thing is true of all these false gods: they will eventually abuse us. Greed devours us; intellectual pursuits lead to arrogance; lovers disappoint us; national leaders fail. But God will never abuse those who serve him. The merciful God of heaven and earth will not mistreat us; he will lift his faithful images to glory.

Why did God insist, "Remember the Sabbath day by keeping it holy" (Ex. 20:8)? This commandment insures that God will be glorified through the worship of his people. But we must not forget Jesus' comment: "The Sabbath was made for man, not man for the Sabbath" (Mark 2:27). The Sabbath was intended not to bind us in chains, but to free us from the bonds that we wrap around ourselves and others. Observing the Sabbath protects us from working ourselves and others to death. The Sabbath is not a curse; it is rest from toil, a gift of refreshment.

All of the commandments of Scripture have the same twofold purpose. They bring glory to God, and they also benefit the image of God. When God spoke, he was not like the careless parent who simply says, "Do what I say because I say so!" Rather, as a loving Father he has told us, "Do what I say because my instructions will make you successful everywhere you go."

The benefit of God's law becomes plain when we see what happens to us when we neglect it. What are the effects on the image of God when we disregard the law of God? Take a look around—it isn't hard to see.

In the 1960s, I shared the belief of many that a new age was on the horizon. "This is the dawning of the Age of Aquarius," we sang. We hoped for the destruction of old power structures and an age of new morality. Freedom from rules, especially those found in the Bible, would bring happiness and fulfillment to the human race.

The package we prepared in those days looked good at the time, but it has begun to unravel in the last twenty-five years. We proclaimed the Age of Aquarius, but we got the Age of AIDS. We looked for an era of free love, but we founded the era of rampant divorce. We expected an epoch of happiness, but we hurled ourselves into an epoch of countless horrors.

Throughout history, God's words to Joshua have proved to be true. The law of God shows us how to fight our battles successfully. Just as it brought material blessings to Joshua in the land of Canaan, so also it points out to us the way to spiritual blessings. God's Word is good; we can have strength and courage in our battles when we follow the reliable guide of Scripture.

GOD'S INTIMATE PRESENCE

"I have no time for friends," the young man thought to himself. "Building relationships takes time that I just don't have."

Isn't that the way many of us feel? Personal relationships are the first casualties of a busy life. Projects so fill our schedules that we have no time for solid friendships. Activities consume our whole lives. We grow impersonal and cold toward others, even those whom we love dearly.

A similar difficulty often plagues Christians in their fight for dignity. Christians who take their call to spiritual warfare seriously have plenty to do. One project after another fills their days. Abortion, pornography, human rights, help for the poor, careers, children, homes, personal struggles—the list is endless. So many battles call for our attention that we sacrifice relationships. Friendships die; children are neglected; marriages fall apart.

As easy as it is to neglect human relationships, it is even easier to disregard our relationship with God. Intimacy with God is often the very first thing we lose when we concentrate on fighting for dignity. We become so preoccupied with serving God that we actually lose personal contact with him. We fight *for* God, but we fight *without* him.

The Lord drew attention to this problem as he addressed Joshua: "Have I not commanded you? Be strong and courageous. Do not be terrified; do not be discouraged, for the LORD your God will be with you wherever you go" (Josh. 1:9).

In this verse, God commanded Joshua for the third time to be strong and courageous, but instead of focusing on the need for a purpose and guide, he assured the warrior of his abiding presence. Joshua could have strength and courage only as he lived in the full assurance that God would be with him wherever he went.

To understand God's instructions to Joshua, we must see how this theme flowed directly from Moses' legacy. The biblical portrait of Moses' life indicates that all three of God's exhortations to Joshua stemmed from Moses' ministry.

Consider the Book of Exodus. It divides into three main sections: Moses' deliverance of Israel (1:1–18:27), Moses' law (19:1–24:18), and Moses' tabernacle (25:1–40:38). The Book of Exodus focuses on the three themes that God presented to Joshua: the purpose of God's people, the law to guide them, and worship in the special presence of God.

With this background in mind, we can understand God's final exhortation to Joshua more clearly. When he told Joshua, "The LORD your God will be with you wherever you go" (Josh. 1:9), he was not calling attention to his omnipresence. He was not merely assuring Joshua that his providential control extended to the land of Canaan. That was true enough, but he had something much more profound in view. God was speaking of Joshua's *experience* of his presence through the worship, sacrifice, and prayer taking place at the tabernacle. "I will be with you" meant "My special presence will always be available to you in the tabernacle."

Now we can see what Joshua had to do for strength and courage. He could face the battles ahead only as he nurtured his fellowship with God. He needed regular experiences of God's presence to face his battles for dignity.

I remember watching a father and his young daughter at the local swimming pool. The seven-year-old was fascinated by teenagers jumping off the high diving board. I could not tell exactly what the father said, but somehow he talked his little girl into trying it for herself. She stood in the long line eagerly waiting her turn. Finally, she reached the top of the ladder and walked out to the edge of the board. When she looked down at the water, however, her countenance fell. The expression on her face betrayed the fear in her heart. She became so frightened that she went back down the ladder, forcing all the teenagers behind her to climb down as well. Enduring their cruel comments, she made her way back to her father in tears.

After a few moments, the father talked his daughter into trying it again. Apparently he promised that he would get into the water and help her when she jumped. The little girl stood in line and finally reached the top again. She walked out to the edge of the board and looked down at the water. It was still a long way down. She looked over at her father, who was now in the water, and motioned for him to come closer. Once he moved into the middle of the pool, she walked back on the board, ran as fast as she could, and jumped right on top of her waiting father.

What gave that little girl the courage to jump? The diving board was just as high. The jump was still a great challenge. What was different the second time around? The girl gained courage to jump because she could see that her father was right there waiting to help her.

In much the same way, Joshua faced a life full of dangers. The battles ahead of him presented all kinds of threats to his safety. Knowing the omnipresence of God was some comfort to the warrior, but courage and strength came only as Joshua was experientially assured that God was right there waiting to help him. Joshua had to devote himself to personal fellowship with God.

If you realize how difficult your spiritual battles are, you also know how important it is to be assured of God's personal attention. The wars ahead are beyond your abilities; you are simply too weak in yourself. The only way to face the difficulties ahead is to bathe yourself in the experience of God's presence.

Just as Joshua had to avail himself of the tabernacle services, we must be warriors who maintain a central place for prayer and worship. We must resist the tyranny of activism by making room for intimate communion with God.

Christians go to extremes in these matters. Some believers are so pietistic that they have little practicality about themselves. They spend so much of their time in prayer and meditation that they don't know when to get off their knees and go to work. Other believers, however, become so involved with doing things, that they have little or no time for communion with God.

God's words to Joshua address both of these extremes. His concern with Joshua's purpose and guidance counters pious passivity. To be strong and courageous in our warfare, we must be ready to act. But God's final exhortation addresses the extreme of activism. We must make prayer and worship central to all of our efforts.

This aspect of spiritual warfare has always been difficult for me. When I first became a believer, nothing was more important than drawing near to Christ in worship. I turned quickly to him with my needs and enjoyed praising him for his goodness. As the years went by, however, the focus of my religious life moved toward other things. I concentrated on learning theology and devoted myself to numerous Christian activities. I studied Christ and served him with zeal, but I nearly lost all personal contact with him. I am happy to say that I have moved back to more devotion and intimacy with Christ in recent years, but for a long time I had lost sight of developing a relationship with him.

I have met countless believers who have gone through similar experiences. Without intending to do wrong, they crowd their lives with so many worthwhile Christian activities that they lose their first love for Christ himself. Invariably, at some point these believers find the weight of their tasks unbearable. They give way to discouragement and defeat.

How can we overcome these difficulties? God's third instruction to Joshua points to the way. Sincere devotion to the presence of God is essential for courage and strength in the Christian life.

What priority do you give to developing your personal experience of God? God warned Joshua not to neglect this aspect of life. If we neglect it, the negative results will eventually take their toll. When we enter battle, we will face defeat. By knowing God's presence in an intimate and dynamic way, we can find the assurance of his care and move forward into the greatest battles.

CONCLUSION

In this chapter we have explored the blessings God gave his image through Moses. God has called us to fight a spiritual war against powerful foes. As he told Joshua, we can find strength and courage for this warfare if we hold on to God's purpose for our lives, his reliable guide in Scripture, and his intimate presence through prayer and worship. By these means we will find ourselves moving toward our

full restoration as images of God. We will discover the way
to fight and win.

28   28   28

REVIEW QUESTIONS

1. How does Joshua's call to war parallel our call to war as
   Christians? How was his warfare different from ours?
2. Why did God connect Joshua's strength and courage
   with the warrior's specific purpose in life? In what ways
   should we focus anew on our purpose in life?
3. How was God's word a reliable guide for Joshua? How
   does God's outlook on his law differ from the ways we
   normally look at his instructions?
4. Why did Joshua need to experience God's presence?
   Why should we nurture the experience of God in our
   day?

DISCUSSION EXERCISES

1. Why is this chapter entitled "Fighting to Win"?
2. Make a list of ten spiritual struggles that require you to
   fight. Why do you need strength and courage for these
   battles?
3. Describe two Christians you know: one who has a clear
   purpose in life and one who does not. How would you
   compare their lives?
4. Examine the Ten Commandments. How does each one
   protect and enhance life for God's image?
5. Why is it difficult for you to nurture your personal relationship with God? Name three specific ways you can
   improve this aspect of your Christian life.

7

CELEBRATING OUR BLESSINGS

During my first year of teaching, I played so much basketball that some of my students nicknamed me "the professor of basketball." Years ago, it wasn't hard to keep up with the guys. I could run up and down the court without much trouble. But as time passed, each new class became faster and faster. Of course, they didn't actually improve that much; the truth is that I was growing older and slower.

As my athletic abilities have declined, my standard for personal success on the court has also dropped significantly. I used to get excited when I had a high-scoring game. Now it is a big deal if I score a few points. I celebrate each basket as if I had just won the game single-handedly.

Most of the fellows understand my enthusiasm, but on one occasion a student took offense at my cheering. "What's the big deal?" he snapped. "You only made one basket."

"Yeah," I said, feeling a little embarrassed. "But when you get as old as I am, you'll celebrate every basket you make, too."

In this chapter we will look into celebration. Throughout this book we have explored God's plan to restore his people to dignity. He gave Noah and his descendants the opportunity to live in a stable world. He showed Abraham and all his chosen people how to reach the goal of restoration. Through Moses, God prepared his people to battle for dignity. Now we will look at the reign of King David, a time when God's people had plenty of reason to celebrate.

As we consider the biblical record of David's life, many issues move to the foreground. We will focus on David's celebration of God's blessings in his life. In David's day, God bestowed countless gifts of dignity on the king and his nation. The Lord took his people a step further from the curse of sin and gave them spectacular honor as his images. From David's reaction to these gifts we will learn how to celebrate God's blessings of dignity in our lives.

DAVID'S KINGSHIP

Kings fill the pages of history books: nobles of Mesopotamia, pharaohs of Egypt, caesars of Rome. Countless royal figures have made great names for themselves. From a biblical perspective, however, no human king has played a more vital role in the history of the world than David, the king of Israel.

Everyone familiar with the Bible knows about David. He was a humble shepherd and obedient son. He showed great courage in battle. He conquered his enemies and provided security for Israel. Nevertheless, these impressive accomplishments do not lift David above all others.

Why does the Bible raise David to the pinnacle of human kingship? What makes him unique? In short, it was not what David did, but what God did for David.

Just as God made covenants at previous points along the road to dignity, he extended a special covenant relationship to David as well. As we have seen, the covenants with Noah, Abraham, and Moses emphasized different aspects of God's plan to redeem his people. In the case of David, God established another covenant that lifted his people to new heights of honor.

The basic elements of God's covenant with David appear in 2 Samuel 7:8–16 (see also 1 Chron. 17:7–14). When David expressed his desire to build a temple for God, Nathan the prophet initially gave his approval (2 Sam. 7:1–3), but during the night God told Nathan that David should not erect a temple (vv. 4–16). Instead, God would build a house for David: "The LORD declares to you that the LORD himself will establish a house for you" (v. 11).

As this verse indicates, the "house" that God would build for David was a dynasty—descendants who would sit on his throne. David's son, Solomon, was to build a temple for the Lord, and God would "establish the throne of his kingdom forever" (vv. 12–13). God swore by solemn oath that David's dynasty would never end.

God knew that David and his descendants would not be perfect, so he made provision for their failures: "I will be his father, and he will be my son. When he does wrong, I will punish him with the rod of men, with floggings inflicted by men. But my love will never be taken away from him, as I took it away from Saul, whom I removed from before you. Your house and your kingdom will endure forever before me; your throne will be established forever" (2 Sam. 7:14–16). When David's descendants rebelled, they would be punished. Human enemies would chastise them.

Nevertheless, God swore that he would never utterly reject David's family. David would always have an heir to sit on the throne. Absolutely nothing would keep this from happening; even defeat and exile could not bring an end to David's dynasty.

God's promise to David brought many blessings to Israel. The establishment of a permanent dynasty advanced the nation's multiplication and dominion. David and his descendants secured a land where Israel's population increased. Dominion over the land was enhanced as the nation prospered. With each of these blessings, Israel experienced significant gains in the process of restoration.

How did David react to God's grace in his life? How did he respond to these gains in dignity? Time and time again, David's heart was filled with exuberant joy. He celebrated his dignity as God's image. One example of David's joy can be found in the Eighth Psalm. As we look at this psalm, we will discover that David celebrated because he understood three things: God at work, our insignificance, and the value of our blessings (see Figure 7).

David's
Celebration

Our
Celebration

God at Work
Our Insignificance
Our Valuable Blessings

Figure 7. Celebrating God's Blessings

RECOGNIZING GOD AT WORK

"How are you doing?" I asked my longtime friend. "How's your daughter?" The last time we had seen each other, they were going through a rough time. Teenage rebellion had stretched their relationship to the limits.

"You wouldn't believe it," the mother said with a big grin. "When Debbie went off to college, my I.Q. skyrocketed; I immediately became a wonderful mother. I don't know how it happened, but I changed completely in just a few weeks!"

Of course, she was being facetious. My friend had not changed a bit. As often happens, moving away from home had shocked her daughter into reality. All of a sudden, she stopped taking Mom for granted. When she began to realize all that her mother had done through the years, her appreciation grew by leaps and bounds.

Christians go through similar experiences with God. We easily overlook how much God has done for us. We go through our daily routines with little appreciation for him, but every now and then something happens that brings us back to reality. We recognize anew that the Lord has been at work in our lives, and our hearts swell with gratitude.

David began his celebration in Psalm 8 with a renewed awareness of God. He turned to his Maker and said, "O LORD, our Lord, how majestic is your name in all the earth!" (Ps. 8:1). If we were to put this verse into modern language, it might read something like this: "Lord, you are so awesome; you have put your name up in lights for everyone to see!" As far as David was concerned, God had done something that caused his name to flash across the heavenly marquee.

Why was David so excited? What had God done? We cannot know precisely, but a couple of hints appear in the second verse of the psalm: "From the lips of children and infants you have ordained praise because of your enemies, to silence the foe and the avenger." The terms "enemy," "foe," and "avenger" suggest that David may have been celebrating a military victory. Perhaps he was returning from battle when this song first rang out. The scene may have been a victory parade where "children and infants" added their voices to the jubilant shouts of their parents.

Whatever the specific circumstances may have been, David had experienced a significant gain in his life, and he began his celebration by boldly announcing that his success was an act of God. He did not look at his victory as a human accomplishment; he did not reduce it to an earthly affair. He attributed his triumph entirely to God.

As we reflect on David's words, it becomes apparent that his attitude contrasts sharply with the way we usually think about our lives. What would you and I have said in David's situation? Most of us have to admit that our first response would have been to pat ourselves on the back and say, "Boy, was I ever lucky!" Perhaps we would go home and declare, "I did a pretty good job today, didn't I?" Unlike David, modern believers often hesitate to acknowledge events as acts of God. Our natural response is to explain things in creaturely terms.

Why is it so natural for us to react in this way? The answer is not that God is inactive. Rather, the problem is that we have developed bad habits. We live in a time when people around us explain as much as they can by ordinary, earthly causes. Modern people spurn mythology and superstition. The world gives credit to God only if no other explanation is available. What are "acts of God" for us? They are tornadoes, earthquakes, floods, and other natural disasters mentioned in the fine print of insurance policies.

These secular outlooks have not remained outside the church. They have also infected God's people. We may not boldly reject the doctrine of a living, active God, but we seldom take the idea very seriously. We push God into the background of insignificance. How many times have you smirked when someone kept telling you, "God did this" and "The Lord did that"? Only old-fashioned fanatics talk that way. Modern, sophisticated believers have a more reasonable approach.

When you give an explanation of an event, what is your first thought? Why do farmers' crops grow? Unless we are talking to young children, we don't usually speak of God. We talk about the many things farmers do to insure a good harvest. Why do we succeed in school? Not because God has taught us, but because we studied. Why do some people enjoy good health? Not because God has given them that gift, but because they eat right and take care of themselves.

It is not wrong to acknowledge the means by which God causes events to take place. He usually works through secondary causes. Yet, we have to be careful not to succumb to the superficial perception of the world. Believers must never be satisfied with looking only on the surface of events. We must also acknowledge the hand of God behind our experiences.

Scripture teaches that God controls everything in our lives. Nothing occurs apart from his wise and holy providence. As we read in Isaiah, "I form the light and create darkness, I bring prosperity and create disaster; I, the LORD, do all these things" (Isa. 45:7). Paul described God as the one "who works out everything in conformity with the purpose of his will" (Eph. 1:11). Christians generally affirm that God's providence involves all facets of their lives. We know this theoretically. But you and I have a long way to go when it comes to applying this belief to daily experience.

While I was writing this chapter, I had a serious automobile accident. I lost control of a friend's car, slammed into a telephone pole, and rolled the car over on its side. The car was mangled, but I climbed out with only a couple of bruises. Two men living near the scene of the accident rushed from their homes to help me out of the car. They saw that I was not hurt, and one of them exclaimed in amazement, "Man, somebody was watching out for you! There's no way you should have lived through that!"

"Someone was watching out for me," I thought to myself. "Yes, God was!" I have thanked him many times for his protection on that dreadful day.

Nevertheless, I have to admit that the lesson I learned that morning didn't stick with me for long. I drove my car with a keen awareness of God's protection for a couple of days. But soon I began to behave just like I used to, never thinking much about God. I know the theological truth that God is in complete control every time I sit behind a steering wheel, but I usually drive without a second thought about his providential hand. That's the way it is for most of us. We drive the car, go to work, eat, sleep, and play, seldom acknowledging that God is working in our lives.

It's to be expected that our awareness of God's actions will vary in intensity from time to time. Even David did not spend every moment feeling overwhelmed by the hand of God. But a serious danger threatens if we consistently fail to acknowledge God's blessings. Without reflecting on God's goodness, we rob ourselves of the joy of knowing how much he cares for us. Deprived of that assurance, we will never be able to celebrate as David did.

I know a man who talks about his mother and grandmother all the time, but never says anything about his father. One day I mustered the courage to ask him about his dad. "Did you have a father?" I asked. "Tell me about him."

"Yeah, I had a father," he replied. "But he wasn't much of a father. He never did anything with me. I don't talk about him because he may as well have been dead."

How sad it is for a child to feel that way about his father. But you and I come close to the same attitude toward our heavenly Father. When we fail to acknowledge God's involvement in our lives, he may as well be dead. Who needs a God like that? How can we celebrate before a God who does nothing?

When was the last time you were utterly overwhelmed by something that God had done for you? Of course, we begin our prayers with the perfunctory, "Thank you for this day and the many other blessings you have given us." But when was the last time you rejoiced from deep within your heart because you knew that God had acted in your life?

A few years ago, I met a man who suffered from a degenerative disease that left him unable to control his limbs and speech. His only means of communication was a computerized voice simulator that constructed simple sentences as he managed to touch the appropriate keys. We sat together one afternoon and I was amazed at how many times this man told me about God's blessings in his life. He went on and on. With every excuse to do otherwise, this fellow praised his God for gifts that gave him tastes of dignity. If a man in that condition can see the hand of God, surely you and I could acknowledge him more.

Think about the events that occurred in your life yesterday. What did you do in the morning and afternoon? What happened in the evening? Now look again and find the kind, caring hand of God in those activities. Acknowledge those events for what they really are—loving acts of God. How was God kind to you? How was he merciful? Follow David's example and tell God how he put his name up in lights for you.

From the opening verses of Psalm 8, we learn a foundational principle for celebrating our dignity as God's image. It is that rejoicing begins with the conviction that God is alive and doing things for us. Only as we see him at work will we be filled with excitement and celebration.

RECOGNIZING OUR INSIGNIFICANCE

I once heard a story about a bank teller in a small town on the West Coast. He met all kinds of people every day, but one afternoon he stared right into the face of his favorite movie star. The teller swallowed deeply as he struggled to greet the celebrity. "M–m–may I h–h–help you?" he finally asked.

The beautiful young woman explained how she had lost her purse and credit cards. Naturally, he dropped everything and scrambled to help her. As the star turned to leave, she stopped and shook the fellow's hand. "Thank you so much," she said. "I don't know what I would have done without you."

The teller stood there in disbelief, staring at his hand. "I can't believe she touched me!" he shouted to his fellow workers. "I'll never wash this hand again!"

Why was this man so excited? He shook hands with people every day. Why did he promise never to wash his hand again? We all know the reason. He could not get over the fact that such a famous person had touched an insignificant person like him.

David's celebration in Psalm 8 reflects a similar perspective. As we have seen, David knew that he had received a blessing from God. But why was he so enthusiastic? Good things happened to him every day of his life. His excitement did not stem from the uniqueness of the event itself. He was celebrating because he realized that God had acted for him—a lowly, insignificant speck of dust. Notice how he put it: "When I consider your heavens, the work of your fingers, the moon and the stars, which you have set in place, what is man that you are mindful of him, the son of man that you care for him?" (Ps. 8:3–4).

David realized something about himself as he gazed at the magnificent moon and stars: "If these things are just the works of God's fingers, who am I that God should care for someone like me?" The celestial bodies were spectacular and David was so insignificant. Nonetheless, God had paid personal attention to him.

David's outlook contrasts with the way we usually think about ourselves. We do not normally walk around contemplating how insignificant we are. Rather, we usually act as if we were the center of the universe.

Let me ask you a question I often ask audiences to whom I speak. Was last week a good week or a bad week? When I ask this question of groups, I usually get mixed responses. Some say it was great; others say it was terrible. But let me ask you another question. How did you decide what to say? What criterion did you use to evaluate those days? Whether we realize it or not, we answer with only one thought in mind. Last week was good if it was good *for me.* It was bad if it was bad *for me.*

Now step back and take another look at last week. It may have been good for you, but it was not good for parents spending night after night beside their daughter's deathbed. The young man suffering from leukemia did not have a good week. It was not positive for your Christian brothers and sisters who were suffering persecution. Yet, when evaluating last week, we ignore what happened to oth-

124

ers and simply consider what happened in our own lives. We all live as if the whole world revolved around us.

As egocentric as we are, every once in a while we catch a glimpse of our insignificance. David looked at the moon and stars and exclaimed, "What is man that you are mindful of him . . . ?" (Ps. 8:3). We face our insignificance when we stand on the edge of the Grand Canyon. "Look how big it is!" we say to each other. Our heads spin as we strain to see the tops of skyscrapers in Manhattan. We understand what we really are when we look out of an airplane and see all the tiny people below.

My wife loves to walk through old cemeteries and search out interesting headstones. One afternoon we strolled through a graveyard in downtown Boston, admiring the winged skulls etched on many early New England tombstones. As I stared at those markers, a somber thought came to me. "All the people here thought they were important, just as we do," I said to my wife. "They all acted as if the world revolved around them, just as we do. But look at them now." Those people thought they were central to the universe, but today their bodies rot away. They were not so important after all. Nor are we.

Do you realize that most people don't even know the first names of their great-grandparents? Your great-grandchildren will probably not know your name, either. How quickly all memory of you will fade from the world. The universe does not revolve around you or me; it hardly knows we are here. This is how small we are.

Wait a minute! I thought we were talking about celebrating our dignity, not lamenting our insignificance. It may sound strange, but David knew something that we often forget. To celebrate our honor as the image of God, we must first understand how small we really are. Until we realize that we are not the center of the world, we will not be able to appreciate how high God's blessings have lifted us.

A number of years ago, a believer from another country gave me a sharp rebuke. "You Americans complain when you have to eat hamburger instead of steak," he said. "You moan when you can't buy a new car. You feel cheated if you can't live in a bigger house. You think so much of yourselves that you can't see how much God has already blessed you! You Americans are spoiled brats!"

That evening I learned something about myself that I find hard to admit. I am a spoiled brat. Maybe my culture has led me in this direction, or perhaps it is just my own self-centeredness. Whatever the reason, I find it hard to rejoice enthusiastically over blessings in my life, because I think I deserve better. Like a spoiled brat, I yawn when I see what God does for me.

As I have visited many churches, I have become convinced that I am not the only ungrateful child of God. Many of us are prone to act like unappreciative children. No wonder we become so dull in our worship; no wonder we sing hymns of praise as if they were dirges; no wonder we offer prayers of thanksgiving in solemn monotone. When we fill ourselves with empty conceit, God's blessings will always seem trivial.

To be people who celebrate their nobility as God's image, we must recognize how insignificant we are in ourselves. We must cry out, "What am I that you are mindful of *me?*"

Consider the gifts that you usually take for granted: good health, faithful children, the church, the Bible, salvation in Christ. These blessings are not beneath us; they are far above us. Only when we recognize how undeserving we are, will we be able to celebrate God's gifts with immeasurable enthusiasm and joy.

RECOGNIZING THE VALUE OF OUR BLESSINGS

Bob walked into his office in dismay, mumbling to himself as he went to his desk: "I'm so stupid. . . . I'm so stupid."

"What's wrong, Bob?" his secretary asked.

"I sold my mother's old ring yesterday for a thousand dollars," he explained.

"I thought you wanted to sell it," she replied.

"Yeah, but during lunch today the buyer came by and told me that the ring was appraised at five thousand dollars! I could kick myself!"

Sometimes we are surprised to see how much an accurate appraisal differs from our own assessment of an item's value. Something may not be worth much in our eyes, but still be priceless. We may believe it is valuable and find out it is actually worthless. To know for certain how much something is worth, we need an accurate appraisal.

To celebrate blessings in our lives, we must know their value. We must recognize how much they are worth. What value do God's gifts have? How much should we treasure them?

We have already seen that David celebrated because he knew that God was at work in his life, even though he did not deserve his attention. Now we come to the third focus of David's joyous heart. He rejoiced because he realized that God's gifts were priceless crowns of dignity.

David's outlook on God's blessings appears in the third portion of Psalm 8: "You made him a little lower than the heavenly beings and crowned him with glory and honor. You made him ruler over the works of your hands; you put everything under his feet; all flocks and herds, and the beasts of the field, the birds of the air, and the fish of the sea, all that swim the paths of the seas" (vv. 5–8).

These words remind us of two other portions of the Old Testament. They recall the passages in Genesis where God first placed Adam and Eve over creation (1:28) and where he reaffirmed his design for humanity's dominion after the Flood (9:1–7). In both passages God established his images as vice-regents over creation. Why did David refer to these passages as he celebrated his own life?

David's allusions to Genesis reveal how he appraised God's blessings. He compared his own experience as the king of Israel with the honor bestowed on Adam in the beginning and on Noah after the Flood. David knew that the good things in his life were demonstrations of his restoration to dignity. He declared that God was lifting him out of the mire of futility and re-establishing him as vice-regent over creation.

It is no wonder that David's heart overflowed with joy. What could be more delightful than seeing God raise him above the curse of his fallen existence? What could be more glorious than realizing that he had been brought another step closer to the original design for God's image?

Following David's example, we must recognize that God's blessings are not isolated events. Rather, they are part of his larger plan for his redeemed images. Every time we receive gifts from God, they bring us closer to the dignity and honor for which he originally designed us.

As Christians, we have even more to celebrate than David did. The writer of Hebrews tells us that the exaltation of humanity mentioned in Psalm 8 was fulfilled in the resurrection of Christ: "But we see Jesus, who was made a little lower than the angels, now crowned with glory and honor because he suffered death, so that by the grace of God he might taste death for everyone" (Heb. 2:9).

When Jesus was lifted from the grave, he took the position of glory and honor belonging to God's image. You and I are, by faith, united with Christ in his resurrection (Rom. 6:5–10; Eph. 2:6; Phil. 3:10–11) and one day will reign with him. On a daily basis, however, God's blessings grant us foretastes of the crowns we will receive at Christ's return.

My childhood church observed a special tradition honoring our women. When teenage girls memorized a number of Bible verses and spent time in some ministry, they were recognized by the church. The girls dressed in fine evening gowns and processed before the entire congregation. During the service, sparkling crowns were placed on their heads in acknowledgment of their work.

At the age of five, I served as a crown bearer for one of these young women. I walked down the aisle and stood right next to her as they put the glittering crown on her head. I can assure you that the young woman did not yawn with boredom. When the shining tiara came to rest on her long red hair, she was absolutely radiant. Pride and joy shone all over her face. As far as she was concerned, that crown was priceless.

The excitement of that moment stands in sharp contrast to something that happened just a few months ago. I was eating in a fast-food restaurant when a family sat down nearby with paper crowns given to them by the manager. After a few minutes, one of the boys reached up, grabbed his father's crown, and tore it to pieces. As the mother began to scold the child, her husband interrupted her. "Don't worry about it, honey," he said. "It's only paper." The father did not care about his crown; he placed no value on it. It was only paper.

Every time God blesses us, he places a crown on our heads. But how do we treat these crowns? Do we quickly push them aside as cheap paper or do we cherish them as crowns of great value?

Too many Christians treat their blessings like paper crowns. They walk around forlorn and discouraged, barely scraping by. Nothing good ever seems to happen to them; no joys ever fill their hearts. If this is your condition day after day, then hear the words of David. Each gift God gives to you is a crown that lifts you to greater heights of honor as his image. God has bestowed his Spirit on you, the down payment of your future inheritance. That crown is priceless in itself, but God has not stopped there. He has poured out blessings upon blessings: years of good health, financial security, Christian family, churches that preach the gospel, opportunities to serve God and neighbor. All of these and countless other gifts are priceless crowns of honor reserved for you, the glorious image of God.

Take another look at your life. Do you see your crowns? Look to your left and right, behind you and in front of you. Crowns are everywhere. When we see how valuable God's blessings are, we soon realize that honor rains down on us all the time. How can we keep from celebrating when every day is our coronation day?

CONCLUSION

God lifted his fallen image to greater heights of dignity in David's kingdom. From Psalm 8 we see that David recognized what God was doing and celebrated with enthusiasm. We must acknowledge how much God works in our lives, how undeserving we are, and how valuable God's blessings are. Then we too will celebrate the blessings we receive as images of God.

≈ ≈ ≈

REVIEW QUESTIONS

1. Why does the Bible exalt David as the greatest human king in history? What did God do for his people through David?
2. Explain how David acknowledged God's activity in Psalm 8. How would David's words have been different if he were a modern, secular person?
3. What made David feel so small in Psalm 8? How did his humble self-reflection lead to a sense of celebration?
4. How much did David value God's blessings in Psalm 8? How did he relate his personal blessings to the honor given to Adam and Noah?

DISCUSSION EXERCISES

1. Why is this chapter entitled "Celebrating Our Blessings"?
2. List ten things you did this week. Describe them in secular terms. Describe them again in spiritual terms. Which description seems more natural to you? What effect does each description have on you?
3. Name three historical figures who thought they were great. What has happened to demonstrate how small and insignificant they really were? What lessons should you learn about your own insignificance?
4. Take a look around the room. What divine blessings do you see? How do we usually treat them as paper crowns? Discuss how these blessings are actually crowns of gold.

8

LONGING FOR MORE

I love spicy Chinese food; I always order my dishes as hot as they come. One time, however, I went too far. As the waiter set the steaming plate on the table, he warned me, "Don't eat the red peppers." But I didn't pay any attention. I bit into what must have been the hottest pepper in the world. With tears streaming from my eyes, I grabbed for my glass and gulped down all the water. As I continued to eat, I called for more and more refills. The fourth time around, the waiter was obviously perturbed. "I'm sorry," I apologized to him, "but these peppers are just too much."

At that, the waiter walked briskly to the kitchen, returned to our table, and slammed a gallon pitcher of ice water in front of me. "Thanks," I sheepishly assured him, "I think that will do it."

My experience that day reminds me of a spiritual reality all of us face as images of God. In the previous chapters of this book, we saw how Adam and Eve left us all with a burning need for relief from sin's defilement. God provided refreshing drinks in the days of Noah, Abraham, Moses, and David, but these cups of water cannot fully satisfy our longing to be restored to dignity. They leave us thirsting for more. We need a giant pitcher of water—something much more than the Old Testament offers.

In this chapter we will review God's gifts in the Old

Testament to see what effects they have had on human life. All of God's blessings have helped us in many ways, but the treasures of the Old Testament are unable to provide all that we need. They cannot bring us to full restoration as God's images. Instead, they leave us longing for an even greater work of God on our behalf.

TWO EFFECTS OF GOD'S BLESSINGS

About five years ago, a good friend of mine donated a computer to my seminary department. We set aside the old electric typewriter and switched on our first office computer. "Look at how fast it is!" a student commented as he joined in the excitement. It was unbelievable—automatic spell checks, editing with a few keystrokes, printing in just seconds. The day before we were enslaved to liquid paper. Now we had entered the world of electronic word processing. My secretary leaned back in her chair and let out a sigh of relief. "This is going to make my job so much easier," she said.

It wasn't long, however, before our initial excitement dissipated. We stood in front of the same computer a couple of weeks later and wondered what had happened. The stacks of paper had not disappeared; my secretary had less time to relax than ever. I could tell from her face that she wasn't happy.

"What's wrong?" I asked her that afternoon. "I thought the computer would make your work easier."

"I can work faster," she replied. "But you've made up for that by giving me more work to do."

Computers can have two effects on office work. They can make us happy by speeding up production, but they can also increase our workload. If we are not careful to handle them properly, computers can actually make life miserable.

In much the same way, God's gifts in the Old Testament produce positive and negative results in our lives. God designed his blessings in the days of Noah, Abraham,

Moses, and David to enhance our dignity; they move us forward in our call to multiplication and dominion. But if we are not careful to handle these gifts properly, they can end up harming us. Instead of helping us reach our goal as images of God, they can cast us deeper into ignobility.

Paul discussed this two-sided outlook on Old Testament blessings in the seventh chapter of Romans. This passage focuses specifically on the Law of Moses, but it offers a perspective that applies to the rest of God's gifts as well.

To understand Paul's viewpoint, we must begin with his positive endorsement of the law. He vigorously denied that the law was flawed. "What shall we say then? Is the law sin? Certainly not!" (Rom. 7:7). God's gift through Moses was a precious treasure: "The law is holy, and the commandment is holy, righteous and good" (v. 12). God "intended to bring life" (v. 10) through the law, and Paul rightly took "delight" in it (v. 22). Paul affirmed the age-old judgment of the psalmist: "The law of the LORD is perfect, reviving the soul. The statutes of the LORD are trustworthy, making wise the simple. . . . They are more precious than gold, than much pure gold; they are sweeter than honey, than honey from the comb" (Ps. 19:7, 10).

What were the effects of this benevolence toward humanity? How did the law influence human life? It had positive and negative effects. On the one hand, it steered us away from sin's destruction: "Indeed I would not have known what sin was except through the law. For I would not have known what coveting really was if the law had not said, 'Do not covet'" (Rom. 7:7). Sin renders human beings spiritually blind, unable to distinguish good from evil on their own. The law helps us identify sin. It warns us against actions and attitudes that harm us, and it directs us toward fruitful living.

The benefits of Moses' precepts become obvious when we look at what happens when people ignore them. Does murder enhance our lives? Does immorality strengthen our character? Does serving idols lift us to higher planes of ex-

135

istence? Of course not. We need the law to guide us through life. It turns the spotlight of God's moral perfection on a world full of darkness. The radiance of the law helps God's image find the path to wise living. Whatever else we may say, we must always remember that the Law of Moses has brought many positive blessings to the world.

On the other hand, the law had negative consequences. Instead of bringing life as God intended, it "actually brought death" (Rom. 7:10). The guide to blessings became a curse.

What happened? How could laws that were sweeter than honey turn so bitter? The Law of Moses became a curse because sinful people abused it. Paul put it this way: "For I would not have known what coveting really was if the law had not said, 'Do not covet.' But sin, seizing the opportunity afforded by the commandment, produced in me every kind of covetous desire. For apart from law, sin is dead" (Rom. 7:7–8).

We need God's law to distinguish good from evil, but trouble begins once we understand the difference between right and wrong. We see the way we should go, but sin works evil in our hearts. The more clearly we know what is good, the more we find ourselves tempted to go in the opposite direction.

In many respects, the Law of Moses is like a "Wet Paint" sign. Painters put up their signs to protect both their work and our clothes. If we obey them, we will be happy; if we disregard them, we will be sorry. God gave his law for the same reason. He posted his moral requirements to warn us against the dangers of sin and to show the way to honorable living.

But what happens when we see "Wet Paint" signs? Sometimes we heed their warning and stay away. But more often than not, an inexplicable curiosity comes over us. We stop and take notice of walls and doors we would have otherwise ignored. "Look at that bench—is it really wet?" we wonder. "I think I'll check it out." Despite the clear warning, we reach over and touch.

This is how the law has produced negative effects. God gave his law to help us, but as we understand his instructions, we find ourselves drawn into disobedience. Sin comes to life and we break God's rules all the more. Instead of reaping positive benefits from the law's guidance, we move further toward ignobility.

Paul's analysis of the Law of Moses applies to all of God's gifts in the Old Testament. God designed all of them for our benefit, and they help us in remarkable ways. Nevertheless, the manner in which we respond turns them into curses. In our sinful hands, God's wondrous blessings are turned inside out, leaving us in even greater need of grace from God. To understand how this is true of all Old Testament blessings, we will take a look at the two effects of God's gifts through Noah, Abraham, Moses, and David (see Figure 8).

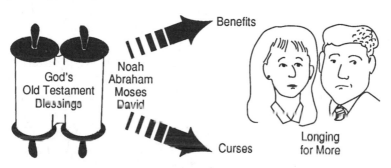

Figure 8. The Effects of Old Testament Blessings

TWO EFFECTS OF NOAH

"I wish I had never given him that car," the desperate mother cried as she sat by her son's casket. A month earlier, she had given her son, Bobby, a used car to drive between his college classes and work. Everything went well for a while, but two days earlier, Bobby had gone out drinking with some friends. On the way home he ran headlong over an embankment and down a fifty-foot cliff. All three men died as the car burst into flames.

"The car was supposed to help him through school," Bobby's mother sobbed. "But look what it did. Look what it did!"

That despairing mother knew that the car she had given her son had made it possible for him to work. But in the final analysis, it did not help Bobby. Her gift actually killed him.

In chapter 4 of this book, we saw that God gave humanity a great opportunity in the days of Noah. Human beings had grossly corrupted themselves, bringing an avalanche of violence upon the world. God cleansed his earth of wickedness, rescued righteous Noah and his family, and graciously formed a stable world where people could live and work as his images. Within the predictable structures of this new natural order, we could work toward successful multiplication and dominion.

What has come of this gift? How has it affected us? When we look around, we see that the stability granted by God has produced two results.

First, God has enabled us to make many positive uses of Noah's blessing. History makes it plain that the predictability of nature has greatly benefited the image of God. All advances in civilization have depended upon the stability that God promised Noah long ago.

We easily forget how much God's covenant with Noah enhances our lives. We grow so accustomed to the order of creation that we act as if it were something automatic, something inherent in nature itself. But as scientists learn more about our world, we see more clearly that the universe is not self-sufficient. Nature is fragile, constantly teetering on the edge of disaster. Disruptions in the food chain, water pollution, atmospheric changes, and the host of other modern environmental concerns demonstrate dramatically that the earth needs the constant providential care of the Creator. The food we eat, the air we breathe, the streets we walk, the cars we drive, the books we read, the buildings we erect, the universities we establish—all of these good things in life have been possible because God constantly upholds a safe place for humanity to multiply and have dominion. As we reflect on God's blessing in the days of Noah, we should be utterly amazed at its tremendous value.

Nonetheless, God's covenant with Noah had a second result. God gave this stable world to sinful people. We have not merely used his blessing—we have also abused it. As a result, the order of nature has also become a curse to us.

The simplest way we pervert God's gift is to waste it. The regularity of life lulls us into complacency. We treat time like a plentiful commodity. "Why do today what you can do tomorrow?" we ask.

I just received notice that my twentieth high school reunion is next year. "Impossible!" I thought to myself. "I can't be that old!" Despite my protests, it is true. Life speeds by like a supersonic jet. As I near the age of forty, it has become increasingly clear to me that time is a precious commodity. God did not give us time in this stable world for us to waste it. He expects us to use our brief lives to serve him to our fullest capacity.

But wasting time is not our worst problem. We could deal with that. Our mishandling of God's gift to Noah goes further. We not only fail to use our opportunity, but also vigorously misuse it. We take the regularity of life as an opportunity to invent ways to bring ignobility upon ourselves.

Seventeenth-century Europe gave birth to the philosophical movement known as the Enlightenment. The scientific advances of the time made the order and predictability of the universe central to human learning. Optimism about the future grew as scientific investigations of the world yielded grand results. A rational, scientific utopia was on the horizon for humanity.

Since the seventeenth century, many philosophical changes have taken place in the West, but one assumption of the Enlightenment has remained very popular. Most people still attach their hopes for humanity to the regularity of nature. The solutions to our troubles lie in working with the natural order of the world. The more we unearth and manage its potential, the better life will be.

Our modern concern for scientific advancement is important. It is a reflection of God's plan for the human race to have dominion. But we must be wary of naive optimism about the results of our work. God provided a regular, natural order that makes it possible to make advances, but what do we do with this opportunity? We twist it to our own destruction.

I once talked with a Christian doctor who pointed out how medical science often perverts the stability of nature. "Did you know," he asked, "that we use the very same knowledge to nurture life in the womb and to destroy it? Advances in prenatal care have also led to more effective abortion techniques. The more we learn for good, the more we have to use for evil."

A similar analysis applies to every area of human culture. The same skills that create musical masterpieces also produce the degrading spectacles of vulgar music videos. The technology that gives us nuclear energy also yields weapons of mass destruction. If we are honest as we look around ourselves, we have to admit that in one way or another, advances in culture also have negative consequences. We use God's orderly world to invent ways to corrupt ourselves.

God's gift to Noah was good. It has benefited us in many ways. But the order of the universe is not enough to make us what God designed us to be. We waste and pervert our opportunities. For this reason, we must look beyond the order of nature to find restoration to dignity as the image of God. God's gift to Noah leaves us longing for more.

TWO EFFECTS OF ABRAHAM

Joey had lots of privileges—he was the pastor's son. He got to stand in the pulpit and pretend to preach. He played the sanctuary organ anytime he wanted. He shot baskets in the church gym every evening. It was great to be the pastor's kid.

But one day Joey abused his privilege. "Come on," he whispered to his buddies standing under the street light. "My dad's the preacher. It's all right."

The boys climbed in the church window and went on a rampage. They hurled hymnals at each other, turned the pulpit on its side, and went swimming in the baptismal pool. As the boys raced through the front hall screaming at the tops of their voices, the doors of the church suddenly flew open. There stood Joey's father.

"You're in big trouble, boys," the pastor shouted as he stared at the youngsters.

"Not me! Right, Dad?" Joey asked with confidence.

"Joey, you're in more trouble than anyone."

"But I'm your son," Joey protested.

"Yes, you're my son," his father conceded. "That's why you should have known better."

Joey learned a hard lesson that day. To be the pastor's son brought him many privileges, but when he abused those privileges, he got into serious trouble.

We looked at the life of Abraham in chapter 5 and saw that he also received a special privilege. God chose him and his family to be recipients of something kept secret from other nations. He showed Abraham how to succeed in multiplication and dominion over the earth. Abraham learned the necessity of trusting in divine power, waiting patiently on God, and persevering in faithful service to him.

These revelations were wonderful gifts. They gave Israel the advantage of knowing what every person must do to be restored to dignity. Nevertheless, the effects of this blessing were not entirely positive. Israel's privilege also got her into serious trouble.

★ What positive benefits came from Abraham's special status before God? To begin with, God's choice of Abraham led to the founding of the nation of Israel. Because

141

Abraham responded appropriately to God's requirements, Sarah bore Isaac. Isaac's grandsons became the heads of the twelve tribes of Israel. In just a few generations, the people of God in the Old Testament grew to tremendous numbers. The gift of God's revelation to Abraham resulted in the creation of the Jewish nation.

Beyond this, Israel became God's instrument of redemption for the whole world. As God spoke through Moses, "You yourselves have seen what I did to Egypt, and how I carried you on eagles' wings and brought you to myself. Now if you obey me fully and keep my covenant, then out of all nations you will be my treasured possession. Although the whole earth is mine, you will be for me a kingdom of priests and a holy nation" (Ex. 19:4–6).

All nations of the earth were to learn the ways of God through the witness of Abraham's descendants. If it were not for them, the Gentiles would have been condemned forever to the darkness of paganism.

Throughout the centuries, many people have tried to downplay Israel's role in human history. Instead of being grateful for Abraham's descendants, they have blamed them for their own religious, economic, and social ills. If these ridiculous lies were not so dangerous, they would be laughable. Anti-Semitism certainly has no historical justification. It is spawned by ignorance and stupidity.

In reality, the Jewish nation has brought immeasurable blessings to the world. No doubt, the Jews have not been perfect. They have turned from their God again and again. In fact, the vast majority of Abraham's physical descendants have even rejected his greatest son, Jesus. Yet, the Jewish nation was God's instrument of blessing for the world.

We see the benefits of Abraham's privilege in many aspects of Western culture. We often describe our highest cultural ideals as expressions of a Judeo-Christian heritage. What positive elements in modern society do not stem from this background? Such ideals as justice, freedom, charity, and love have resulted from the special status that Abraham and his descendants enjoyed before God.

Of course, the greatest benefit of God's relationship with Abraham is the gospel itself. We must never forget what other nations were doing when Abraham was circumcising himself in devotion to the true God. My ancestors were worshiping rocks and chasing after demons. What were yours doing? Much the same, I'm sure. But look at you now. Your faith in Christ is proof of how enormously the Jews have blessed the nations of the earth. Jesus, the Savior of the world, came from the line of Abraham. The apostles who spread the gospel were also Jews. The worldwide influence of the gospel resulted from God's revelation to Abraham: "I will bless those who bless you, and whoever curses you I will curse; and all peoples on earth will be blessed through you" (Gen. 12:3). What greater positive result could there be?

Despite these benefits, however, Abraham's blessing also led to failure and curses. His descendants took their privileged place in God's plan as permission to live as they pleased. Nearly every book of the Old Testament testifies to Israel's persistent abuse of her privileges. The people grumbled after God delivered them from Egypt. They disregarded him during the period of the judges. The nation repeatedly fell into apostasy under the kings.

Why did the Jews fail so terribly? The primary cause of Israel's rebellion becomes plain in a scene from the New Testament. When John the Baptist was preparing the way for the Messiah, he preached to Israel, "Repent, for the kingdom of heaven is near" (Matt. 3:2). Many Jews turned back to the Lord, but others refused. What kept them from repentance? The Jews rejected John's warnings because they felt secure as heirs of Abraham's promises. "What do we have to worry about?" they asked each other. "We have God's covenant with Abraham. We are his privileged children."

But John the Baptist vigorously opposed that outlook.

He told them, "Do not begin to say to yourselves, 'We have Abraham as our father.' For I tell you that out of these stones God can raise up children for Abraham" (Luke 3:8).

John warned that unfaithful Jews were in line for severe judgment, not blessing. "The ax is already at the root of the trees, and every tree that does not produce good fruit will be cut down and thrown into the fire" (Luke 3:9). Israel's privilege led to license, license led to sin, and sin led to judgment.

The privileges we enjoy as Christians have caused us to operate with the same presumptions. Countless people drift away from commitment to Christ, fully convinced that they are safe. We encounter this attitude in all of our churches. "I am a church member," one man told me. "I don't have anything to worry about." "I go to church every Sunday," others insist. "I teach Sunday school and sing in the choir," still others say. But we must remember the words of John the Baptist. God can raise up church members from the rocks.

The problem with privilege is that we abuse it. Once we think we are special in God's eyes, we believe we can do anything we want. But nothing could be further from the truth. Presumption will not lead to blessings; it will only bring us under God's judgment.

God's blessings in the days of Abraham were wonderful. They established a privileged people, honored with knowing the way to salvation for God's image. Nevertheless, these privileged people turned their blessings into curses. As much as God gave us in Abraham, the image of God still needs more to reach full restoration to dignity.

TWO EFFECTS OF MOSES

"How do you like your job?" I asked the mechanic as he worked on the brakes of my car.

"Okay," he replied, "but I'll tell you one thing. This

is not the kind of work you do only halfway. If you don't finish this job, you can really hurt somebody."

It doesn't make much difference if you leave some jobs incomplete—cleaning the house, typing a paper. "Half is better than nothing," we say to ourselves as we stop for a break. But we have to finish other tasks or they create serious dangers—brake repairs, electrical wiring, medical procedures.

In the sixth chapter of this book, we looked at a job that the redeemed image of God had to complete. Through Moses' ministry, God prepared Israel to gain victory in war against the Canaanites. This call to conquest was a tremendous blessing for the people of Israel, but it also placed them in a dangerous position. Complete victory would bring them many benefits, but doing this job halfway would bring them harm. For this reason, God showed Joshua how to maintain strength and courage during the conquest of Canaan. Joshua had to remember his purpose in life, follow the Law of Moses, and attend to the presence of God through worship and prayer.

Initially, Israel's campaign was extraordinarily successful. With rare exception, the people of God kept their purpose before them, observed the Law of Moses, and depended on God's presence. As a result, Joshua and the people conquered their enemies and rested in their new homeland. Through their early victories, the people of God found a place where they could multiply and have dominion as never before. In this sense, God brought great benefits to his people.

Despite these blessings, however, Israel reacted to her call to conquest in a way that brought serious harm to the image of God. God had clearly ordered Israel to destroy all of the Canaanites. As he said to Moses, "When the LORD your God has delivered them over to you and you have defeated them, then you must destroy them totally. Make no treaty with them, and show them no mercy" (Deut. 7:2). Those who had defiled the land of Canaan were to be utterly destroyed.

145

After Joshua's death, however, Israel lost sight of the need to complete the conquest. The opening chapters of the Book of Judges tell us what happened (Judg. 1:1–2:5). One after another, the tribes fell short of driving out all of the Canaanites.

The Israelites never completely destroyed their enemies. Had they done so, God's call to war would have been pure blessing for his people. Israel would have experienced unhindered prosperity in the land. But doing this job halfway led to serious problems:

> Therefore the LORD was very angry with Israel and said, "Because this nation has violated the covenant that I laid down for their forefathers and has not listened to me, I will no longer drive out before them any of the nations Joshua left when he died. I will use them to test Israel and see whether they will keep the way of the LORD and walk in it as their forefathers did." The LORD had allowed those nations to remain; he did not drive them out at once by giving them into the hands of Joshua. (Judg. 2:20–23)

When Israel allowed the Canaanites to live in the land, they became a source of trouble. Over the course of time, the evil of the Canaanites infected God's people, and Israel became just like the nations around her. She lost sight of her purpose as God's holy army, turned away from the Law of Moses, and corrupted her worship. In this way, the legacy of God's call to war brought harm to Israel.

Israel's failure in conquest reminds me of a conversation I had with a juvenile probation officer. He lamented a difficult choice he often faced: "The biggest problem I have is sending young boys to the detention center. If they get their minds set in the right direction, it can be the best thing for them. But most of the time the young boys give up on trying to improve themselves. Then they come under the influence of older boys who teach them more ways to break the law."

In a similar way, we often give up on the battles we face. We hear the call to spiritual warfare and move into the world for Christ. But what happens so often when we begin to wage our holy war? We enter the arts, business, civic organizations, and schools to have an influence, but we soon lose sight of the goal. We compromise with the world short of total victory. We lessen our zeal to oppose rebellion against God and find ourselves drawn into the practices of the world. Our families, our businesses, and even our churches are corrupted by the evil influences surrounding us.

The call to conquest was not faulty in itself. Our call to holy war enhances our lives in many ways, but we take this gracious blessing and turn it into a detriment. We must never discard what God did for us through Moses. Yet, we must also recognize that it was not enough to give us a full measure of dignity.

TWO EFFECTS OF DAVID

Roy called his used car lot "My Sons and Me Auto Sales."

"I named the business that," he recalled, "because I was sure my boys would be in the business with me."

Roy's two sons worked for their father for a while. They washed cars after school. During the summers they learned how to make simple repairs. After high school graduation, Roy gave the boys shares in the company and taught them every aspect of the business.

"I gave them a taste of success," Roy said, "and then they turned their backs on me." After only one year, Roy's sons left to start their own car lot down the road. "I gave them so much that they thought they didn't need me anymore," Roy said with a grin. "Then I showed them the difference between being my partners and being my competitors."

Roy's sons had made a big mistake. They became so proud of their quick success that they failed to remember who made their good fortune possible. It was only six months before they learned how difficult it was to be their father's competitors. The boys went bankrupt and lost all they had.

This story reminds us of what God's people did with the blessings of King David. In the seventh chapter of this book, we saw that God loved David with special affection. God gave him enormous riches and established his throne as a permanent dynasty over Israel. God promised David a kingdom of eternal significance. How did these blessings affect the image of God?

On the one hand, God's love for David brought many blessings. He reached into David's life and lifted his kingdom to heights of honor. Victory, prosperity, and fame belonged to David. The king received so much from God that he exclaimed, "You . . . crowned [humanity] with glory and honor" (Ps. 8:5). As David's descendants inherited his throne, they also received many blessings. The nation expanded under Solomon and the fame of his glory spread throughout the world. Israel grew from an insignificant nation to a major power because of the promises made to David.

On the other hand, Israel reacted to David's blessings much as Roy's sons reacted to their father's kindness. Every time the kingdom seemed secure, the kings and their people turned away from God. Forgetting that God had supplied all that they had, the people of Israel relied on the paper-thin security of outward success in this world.

Repeatedly during the reign of David's family, kings rebelled against God when they were successful. David himself turned to Bathsheba at the height of his prosperity; his sin brought the sword to his royal house. Rich and famous

Solomon constructed chapels for the gods of his foreign wives. This sin resulted in the division of the kingdom. King after king took success in his reign as grounds for rebellion against God. Their arrogance became so offensive that God finally sent the people of both the northern kingdom and the southern kingdom into exile.

A common thread runs through all of these events. God's people saw how much they had in this world. The blessings were great—no one could deny that. Yet, the splendor of these gifts led Israel away from her heavenly King. Instead of becoming more grateful, the nation turned away from God to the false security of earthly things.

I remember speaking with a teenager one Sunday afternoon. He was distraught about inconsistencies in his spiritual walk. "I don't know what to do," he confessed. "The only time I want God in my life is when things are bad. I never pray unless I'm in some kind of trouble. I don't want to go to church unless my life is messed up. What's wrong with me?" he asked.

"Something that's wrong with all of us," I replied. "We all tend to forget God when blessings surround us."

We are no different from that young man. Nor are we different from David and his sons. We have received many gifts from God because we are heirs of David's kingdom in Christ. We should rejoice in these blessings and serve God even more faithfully. But how do we usually react to them? Are we moved to gratitude and obedience? Sometimes. But we usually find that our mountains of blessings block our vision of God. The lordship of Christ is hidden from our view. We no longer feel as if we need God.

God's gifts through David had two effects on the image of God. They brought many positive blessings and a glorious kingdom that will never end. Nevertheless, God's work through David's life had negative effects as well. As sinful people, we allow the splendor of God's kingdom to override our devotion to God himself. His rich gifts so captivate our hearts that we lose our sense of dependence on

149

and service to him. For this reason, even God's greatest work on behalf of his image in the Old Testament cannot give us what we need. We must look even beyond David for our full restoration to dignity as the image of God.

CONCLUSION

God did much for his image in the Old Testament. We utterly ruined ourselves through sin, but God reached down in the days of Noah, Abraham, Moses, and David. His gifts have helped us in countless ways; we must never disregard them. But these Old Testament blessings were not enough to restore us to our full dignity as God's image. What do we need beyond these gifts? As we will see in the next chapter, we need the gift of Christ.

৵   ৵   ৵

REVIEW QUESTIONS

1. How can God's gifts have positive and negative effects on the human race? How does this fact cause us to long for more from God?
2. Compare and contrast the benefits and the problems for God's image in the blessings of Noah, Abraham, Moses, and David.

DISCUSSION EXERCISES

1. Why is this chapter entitled "Longing for More"?
2. List five ways in which you fail to make proper use of God's gift of a stable world. How can you change your usual practices?

3. Describe a person who abuses his or her privileges before God. How could he or she avoid this problem?
4. In what area of your life have you not completed the job of spiritual warfare? How have you been compromising with the world?
5. Have you seen yourself (or another person) distracted from devotion to God because you possess so many earthly treasures? How has this happened?

9

TAKING THE LAST STEP

Watch out for the last step," my host warned as we climbed the stairs leading to his front door. "It's bigger than all the others."

It was a long flight of stairs up a steep hill, and I forgot his warning for a moment. But when we reached the top, I saw what he meant. The step just in front of the door was at least three times higher than the others.

"You weren't kidding, were you?" I chuckled as I strained to lift my bags high enough.

"Yeah," he replied, "but it's good to know that this is the last one. Come on in."

Throughout this book we have been climbing the stairs of Scripture that lead to the restoration of God's image. Little by little, God blessed his people with gifts that could move them away from sin's ignobility and closer to the dignity for which he originally designed the human race. As we have seen, these major strides took place in the days of Noah, Abraham, Moses, and David.

In the preceding chapter, however, we noticed that all of God's blessings in the Old Testament leave us longing for more. Although God's gifts in ages past impact our lives in many positive ways, our sinful responses render them unable to restore us to dignity. But now we are in a position to look beyond the Old Testament. We come to the time when God took his image to the last and greatest step, which fully restores us to dignity.

Jesus is the last step in God's plan. God completed the redemption of his image by sending his own Son. To understand what God accomplished through Christ, we will explore how the New Testament compares him with Adam, Noah, Abraham, Moses, and David. As we will see, Christ reversed the fall of Adam and gathered all the blessings of Old Testament history in himself. The work of Christ far exceeded anything God had done beforehand. Christ alone renews us to dignity (see Figure 9).

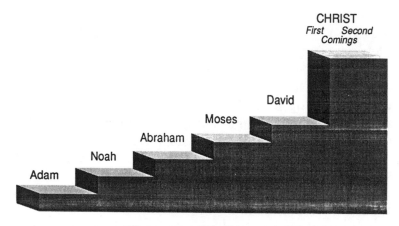

Figure 9. Christ, the Last Step

CHRIST AND ADAM

Mirror images are strange; they look like the objects they reflect, but the image is also reversed. Objects and their reflections have the same contours and colors, but their horizontal directions are reversed. What do you see when you hold a written page in front of a mirror? Left is right and right is left. Mirror images are the same and opposite at the same time.

To understand how Christ restores human dignity, it helps for us to think of him as the mirror image of Adam. The New Testament calls Jesus the "last Adam" (1 Cor. 15:45). He directly corresponds to the first man of creation. As a mirror image, however, Christ is not only like Adam, but also the opposite of Adam.

How is Christ similar to the first man? Many connections exist between the two, but we will mention three important points of comparison. First, both Adam and Christ were perfect images of God. In Genesis, Moses portrayed sinless Adam as God's untainted likeness. In much the same way, Paul described Christ as "the image of God" (2 Cor. 4:4; see also Col. 1:15). As perfect divinity and perfect humanity, Christ uniquely represented God in the world.

Second, Adam and Christ received similar commissions as God's images. God ordained Adam to multiply and have dominion over the earth. He also sent Christ to rule and multiply. Jesus revealed the importance of these goals in his life when he commissioned his disciples (Matt. 28:18–19). Dominion stands out first: "All authority in heaven and on earth has been given to me" (Matt. 28:18). In his resurrection, Christ received authority over all things. In this way, he fulfilled humanity's destiny of dominion. Jesus also mentioned the task of multiplication to his apostles: "Therefore go and make disciples of all nations" (Matt. 28:19). Jesus devoted himself to multiplying redeemed images of God and commissioned his apostles to do the same. Christ multiplied and exercised dominion in ways that exceed all the accomplishments of humanity before or after him.

Third, both Adam and Christ played pivotal roles in human history. As the first image of God, Adam represented all human beings who followed him. His actions were more than personal choices. They had consequences for all of his descendants. As Paul put it, "Sin entered the world through one man, and death through sin, and in this way death came to all men, because all sinned" (Rom.

5:12). As our representative, Adam introduced sin and judgment to the human race.

God also established Christ as a representative of others. His actions were more than personal choices. They had effects on the lives of God's redeemed people: "For if, by the trespass of the one man, death reigned through that one man, how much more will those who receive God's abundant provision of grace and of the gift of righteousness reign in life through the one man, Jesus Christ" (Rom. 5:17). Christ's actions brought righteousness to those who are made anew through faith.

In athletic competitions, coaches do their best to match opponents with comparable players from their own team. They do not usually put a weaker player against a stronger one. If it is possible, coaches want their team members to be equal to, if not better than, their opponents. Otherwise, the team can hardly hope to win.

This principle reveals why Christ alone can fully restore human beings to dignity. Only he is as great as—and even greater than—Adam. Men like Noah, Abraham, Moses, and David played important roles in the redemption of our fallen race. Yet, no one before or after Christ was in a position to be the last Adam. No other person has been the perfect image of God. No one else has fulfilled humanity's task without fault. No other person has represented the host of redeemed humanity in God's eyes. Christ was a new beginning for the human race. He alone could lead us to the full realization of all that God had designed us to be.

Christ's unique superiority over Adam is the reason why all our hopes for dignity rest ultimately in him. Can we trust ourselves to reverse the Fall? Never. We are not Adam's peers in God's eyes. Can we trust other people to redeem us? No. Who among us is able to undo what the first man did? Jesus, the last Adam, is the only man capable of reversing our fall into sin. If we hope to rise above the futility of death, we must look to him.

As Adam's superior, Christ reversed the effects of humanity's fall. Where Adam brought death, Christ brought life. Where Adam caused the curse of ignobility and judgment, Christ produced dignity and salvation.

When did Christ accomplish this restoration? He did not do it all at once. It began during his first appearance on earth, and it will be completed only when he returns.

The initial phase of Christ's restorative work began with his life on earth two thousand years ago. At the beginning of Jesus' ministry, Satan tempted him as he had tempted Adam (Matt. 4:1–11), but Christ resisted: "For we do not have a high priest who is unable to sympathize with our weaknesses, but we have one who has been tempted in every way, just as we are—yet was without sin" (Heb. 4:15). Paul noted this difference between Adam and Christ when he contrasted "the disobedience of the one man" (Adam) with "the obedience of the one man" (Christ) (Rom. 5:19).

Jesus' greatest act of obedience was his death on the cross. Following the Father's command, he suffered the curse placed on Adam (Gen. 3:19). He endured the cross as our representative to bring an end to the curse against us: "But he was pierced for our transgressions, he was crushed for our iniquities; the punishment that brought us peace was upon him, and by his wounds we are healed" (Isa. 53:5).

Beyond this, however, Christ did not remain under the curse of death. The Father resurrected him by the Spirit. As the representative head of the new humanity, he also brought new life to all who believe in him: "If we have been united with him like this in his death, we will certainly also be united with him in his resurrection" (Rom. 6:5).

Just as Christ stepped from the old world of death into the new world of resurrection, we too find newness of life by entrusting ourselves to him. We walk not under God's curse, but under his blessings.

Christ's first appearance on earth dramatically changed the course of human history. His death and resurrection began the last step toward the restoration of God's image. Even so, it should be evident that those who trust Christ for that restoration are not yet fully renewed. We still struggle with sin; we still face death. When will we find complete restoration?

The second coming of Christ is our hope for full redemption as God's images. At the present time, Christ "must reign until he has put all his enemies under his feet" (1 Cor. 15:25). At his return, however, Christ will bring final judgment against the enemies of God. He will receive the rewards he so richly deserves, and the Father will exalt him as the unquestioned ruler of all.

As our representative before God, Christ will not keep all of this glory for himself. He will share the blessings of eternal life with his people: "The first man was of the dust of the earth, the second man from heaven. As was the earthly man, so are those who are of the earth; and as is the man from heaven, so also are those who are of heaven. And just as we have borne the likeness of the earthly man, so shall we bear the likeness of the man from heaven" (1 Cor. 15:47–49).

Christ is the last Adam, the head of a new humanity. He alone has the power to make us whole. He began to reverse the effects of Adam's sin in his life, death, and resurrection, but he will complete his work when he returns to earth for the second time. In this way, Christ is the last step in our restoration to dignity.

CHRIST AND NOAH

"I tried to stop many times," the young man confessed. "Drugs had hurt me and I knew I needed to turn my life around. But as hard as I tried, I could not escape their grip."

Many drug abusers will tell you that they would like to kick the habit. They see the terrible consequences of addiction and try to change their lives.

"Do you know what made the difference in my life?" the young man continued. "One night I tried to kill myself. I was rushed to the hospital and almost died. The doctors barely saved me. At that point my whole life changed. It took something that drastic to turn my life around."

In the days of Noah, as we saw in chapter 4, God gave his image the opportunity to turn away from sin's destruction. He judged wicked humanity, rescued Noah and his family, and gave us a new and stable world. But people failed to take advantage of this opportunity. Noah became drunk after the Flood and his son Ham sexually violated him (Gen. 9:21–22). Humanity did not change; we continued to be addicted to the ways of the past, following paths of ignobility.

Deep in our hearts, we have to wonder if it is possible to overcome our fallen condition. If something as dramatic as a worldwide flood failed to wrench us out of ignobility, how will we ever escape sin's destructive grasp? The New Testament gives us the answer to these perplexing questions. God has provided the way in Christ. He sent his Son into the world to accomplish what the Flood was unable to do.

The apostle Peter drew attention to the connections between Christ and Noah more than any other biblical writer. He explained Christ's significance by comparing him with Noah in two ways. As we look at these passages, we will see how God turned us around by sending Christ. In 1 Peter 3:20–22 we read:

God waited patiently in the days of Noah while the ark was being built. In it only a few people, eight in all, were saved through water, and this water symbolizes baptism that now saves you also—not the removal of dirt from the body but the pledge of a good conscience toward God. It saves you by the resurrection of Jesus Christ, who has gone into heaven and is at God's right hand—with angels, authorities and powers in submission to him.

This passage appears within a larger context dealing with Christian suffering. To assure believers that their suffering was not in vain, Peter referred to the fact that Noah's ark saved some, while the Flood judged the rest of humanity. The thought of rescue and judgment through water drew Peter's thoughts to a fascinating parallel in the earthly ministry of Jesus. Judgment and salvation were also associated with the water of Christian baptism.

The water of baptism serves a purpose similar to that of the water of the Flood. Jesus commanded his apostles to "make disciples of all nations, baptizing them in the name of the Father and of the Son and of the Holy Spirit" (Matt. 28:19). In line with Noah's flood, baptism's design is negative and positive. On the negative side, it judges those who are without Christ. They store up wrath against themselves because they stand opposed to him and refuse to place their faith in him.

On the positive side, baptism represents the cleansing of salvation for believers. Just as the Flood brought Noah and his family into a new world, so baptism now delivers us into a new world of salvation. Baptism itself saves no one; the rite must be a sign of "a good conscience toward God" (1 Peter 3:21). Yet, as God delivered Noah through the waters of the Flood, he delivers his people now through faith, symbolized in the waters of Christian baptism.

Think about what Peter has said about your baptism. Many Christians think of the rite as hardly more than an empty ritual, but this is not the attitude of Scripture. As a sign and seal of saving faith, baptism separates you from a world destined for judgment. Your personal commitment to Christ and your union with him have turned your life

160

around. When we trust in Christ, God floods our world with blessing and carries us into a new world of hope and opportunity.

The salvation represented in Christian baptism is much greater than Noah's deliverance. The ark took Noah and his family into a material world still corrupted by sin. Humanity continued to pursue a course that was contrary to the will of God. But Christ does not deliver us from one corrupt world to another. In Christ we are joined to the glory of his resurrection: "[Baptism] saves you by the resurrection of Jesus Christ, who has gone into heaven and is at God's right hand—with angels, authorities and powers in submission to him" (1 Peter 3:21–22). As Christ was taken to the heights of eternal glory by his resurrection and ascension, so we who are joined to him by faith are taken into that same eternal glory.

For this reason, the work of Christ far exceeds the acts of God in Noah's day. All who trust Christ are taken into a new spiritual world—"our citizenship is in heaven" (Phil. 3:20). Raised with Christ in his resurrection, we have received deliverance from eternal judgment.

Peter also called attention to parallels between Noah's day and the time of Christ's return:

> First of all, you must understand that in the last days scoffers will come, scoffing and following their own evil desires. They will say, "Where is this 'coming' he promised? Ever since our fathers died, everything goes on as it has since the beginning of creation." But they deliberately forget that long ago by God's word the heavens existed and the earth was formed out of water and by water. By these waters also the world of that time was deluged and destroyed. By the same word the present heavens and earth are reserved for fire, being kept for the day of judgment and destruction of ungodly men. (2 Peter 3:3–7)

161

In this passage, Peter answered those who scoffed at the hope of Christ's second coming. These skeptics claimed that everything had been the same since creation (v. 4). "God has not interrupted history before now," they thought. "Why should we think he will in the future?" In response, Peter reminded his readers that the world had not always been the same. God had created the world "out of water and by water" (v. 5), but "the world of that time was deluged and destroyed" (v. 6). History had not continued uninterrupted. God intervened against evil and destroyed the world that he had created. Those who doubt that God would interrupt history at Christ's second coming should take heed. They are warned that "the present heavens and earth are reserved for fire, being kept for the day of judgment and destruction of ungodly men" (v. 7).

Peter drew a direct comparison between Noah's flood and the return of Christ. Just as God dramatically interrupted history in Noah's time, he will intervene even more dramatically by sending Christ back in glory.

As decades, centuries, and millennia pass with little change in the world, it is easy for us to lose hope that things will ever be different. Don't you wonder if God will ever change the world in a dramatic way? We doubt at times, but we can take heart. God did not allow sin to go unpunished in Noah's time; he will not let it go unpunished in the future. He did not fail to rescue his people from judgment in Noah's day; he will not fail to rescue us in the future. Christ certainly will return and bring us into a new heavens and a new earth.

Christ is like Noah, but he also supersedes his Old Testament counterpart. He ordained Christian baptism as a sign of faith that turns our lives away from sin and death. When he returns, a re-creation will take place, where sin will be no more, and the redeemed images of God will be entirely free from ignobility. Unlike Noah, Christ will not give us only a measure of relief from the curse placed on the earth. As the last step of God's plan, he will deliver us completely.

CHRIST AND ABRAHAM

"At last, I have a child!" my buddy cried as we embraced in the hospital hallway. He and his wife had wanted children for a number of years and they finally got their wish. "Now I have an heir," he said with a smile. "I'm going to give him a great inheritance. I may not do much with my life, but he'll be able to do so much more."

Good parents always think about the future of their children. We work hard to pass some kind of inheritance to them. All loving fathers and mothers dream of their children going far beyond what they have accomplished.

In many respects, a similar relationship connects Abraham and Christ. As we saw in chapter 5, the Old Testament Patriarch received wonderful blessings from God. God separated him from the rest of humanity and showed him the power, patience, and perseverance necessary to reach the blessings of dignity. But the Patriarch did not hope in God just for himself. He looked beyond himself to a future heir, one who would go far beyond anything that he could accomplish in his day. This heir was none other than Christ.

The apostle Paul identified Christ as the heir of Abraham's blessings on several occasions. In Galatians 3:16, for instance, he said, "The promises were spoken to Abraham and to his seed. The Scripture does not say 'and to seeds,' meaning many people, but 'and to your seed,' meaning one person, who is Christ." In this passage, Paul indicated that the promise given to Abraham's seed was not simply given generally to his many descendants, but was given particularly to a special Seed. As the extraordinary descendant of Abraham, Christ received the blessings of dignity that had been promised to the Patriarch and the nation of Israel. Abraham's inheritance became the inheritance of Christ.

One aspect of Abraham's inheritance was innumerable descendants. God "took him outside and said, 'Look up at the heavens and count the stars—if indeed you can count

them.' Then he said to him, 'So shall your offspring be'"
(Gen. 15:5). The Patriarch dreamed of the day when his
descendants would be too numerous to count. How was
this promise fulfilled? Abraham experienced the beginnings
of fulfillment in the birth of Isaac. Later on, Israel multiplied into a great nation. But these experiences were over-
shadowed by Israel's apostasy. Abraham had many physical
descendants, but most of them turned away from God. The
spiritual side of Abraham's multiplication ended in ruin.

When we see the continuing rebellion of Israel today,
we have to wonder if the Patriarch's hopes were in vain. Did
Abraham dream of something that would never be? Will redeemed images of God fill the earth—or will they simply
disappear? The New Testament declares that the promise
of multiplication given to Abraham is fulfilled through his
special heir. Christ increases the number of the redeemed
as never before.

At Christ's first coming, the multiplication of Abraham's children took a giant leap forward. Jesus and his apostles accomplished this by adding Gentiles to the remnant
of Israelites who believed in Christ. In the New Testament
period, all believers from every nation are adopted into
Abraham's family:

> Consider Abraham: "He believed God, and it was
> credited to him as righteousness." Understand,
> then, that those who believe are children of Abra-
> ham. The Scripture foresaw that God would justify
> the Gentiles by faith, and announced the gospel in
> advance to Abraham: "All nations will be blessed
> through you." So those who have faith are blessed
> along with Abraham, the man of faith. (Gal. 3:6–9)

So it is that Christ went far beyond what Abraham and
his Old Testament descendants were able to do. By bringing Gentiles into Abraham's family, Christ multiplied the
Patriarch's descendants beyond measure.

At Christ's second coming, however, the multiplication of Abraham's children will be even greater. The Bible offers a striking portrait of humanity in the new heavens and the new earth. Standing before the throne of God will be those adopted into Abraham's family "from every tribe . . . and nation" (Rev. 5:9). When Christ returns, the whole earth will be filled exclusively with Abraham's children.

Another aspect of Abraham's inheritance was the promise of a land. How was this blessing of dignity fulfilled? Abraham himself tasted a bit of this promise as he traveled throughout the land. He gained more of it when he purchased a burial site for his wife (Gen. 25:10). Old Testament Israel saw this promise fulfilled in greater ways through Joshua's conquest and the establishment of David's royal line. Nevertheless, the promise of dominion over the land was not ultimately fulfilled in these events. When Israel turned away from God, she was driven from the land. Relatively few ever returned.

At his first coming, Christ began the process of giving dominion back to Abraham's descendants. He redeemed some Israelites in Palestine and granted them renewed dominion. Yet, Christ went much further. After his resurrection, he told his disciples, "You will receive power when the Holy Spirit comes on you; and you will be my witnesses in Jerusalem, and in all Judea and Samaria, and to the ends of the earth" (Acts 1:8). As the gospel reached into other lands, the influence of Christians spread. The dominion of God's people extended beyond the border of Canaan to all the earth.

At Christ's second coming, the dominion of Abraham's seed will have no bounds. It will extend without exception to the entire planet. At that time the host of heaven will shout, "The kingdom of the world has become the kingdom of our Lord and of his Christ, and he will reign for ever and ever" (Rev. 11:15).

Despite the failures of Israel in the Old Testament, we should not lose hope that Abraham's children will fill the earth and have dominion. Abraham did not see the full extent of God's blessings in his lifetime. Nor did Old Testament Israel experience her potential grandeur. But Christ brings these hopes to fruition. He provides the last step in the restoration of God's image.

CHRIST AND MOSES

During World War II, commanders of the Allied forces strongly disagreed on the strategy that would free Europe from Nazi domination. One general urged his plan of attack; another argued for a different strategy. At times, their differences seriously threatened the unity of the coalition. But in the end, a single plan emerged. It may not have been the strategy desired by all, but the plan for battle led to final victory.

In chapter 6 we saw that God gave Moses the privilege of preparing Israel to conquer the land of Canaan. In a world full of forces opposed to the ways of God, restoration to dignity could come only through warfare. Unfortunately, God's battle plan was different from what many in Israel desired. They expected one strategy, but God dictated another. In the end, however, God's plan of attack led his people to the victory he had promised.

When did the people of God experience this victory? Israel enjoyed small successes on many occasions. The initial successes under Joshua's leadership represented major strides. The defeat of oppressive enemies through the judges brought God's blessings to the nation. The military might of David, Solomon, and other kings of Israel extended the nation's power. God granted his Old Testament people many successes in holy war.

But these victories never reached the heights anticipated by God's promises. In fact, by the end of the Old Testament period, Israel came under the dominion of foreign powers. Babylonians, Persians, Greeks, and Romans ruled the Promised Land for generations. Instead of Israel conquering God's enemies, evil nations conquered Israel.

Between the Old and New Testaments, the people of Israel looked longingly toward a time when God would intervene and grant them the full victory he had promised long before to Moses and Joshua. The New Testament brought good news to those who yearned to see the struggle for dignity completed. Victory in holy war was accomplished by Christ. Sadly, many of the Jews in Jesus' day expected the Messiah to take the throne in Jerusalem and lead them to victory on the battlefield, after which the blessings of God's kingdom would come to earth. When the Messiah appeared, however, his holy war took quite a different form—one unacceptable to most Jews. Jesus did not wage a physical battle with spiritual consequences, as they wanted. Rather, he fought a spiritual war with delayed physical consequences.

At his first coming, Christ initiated spiritual holy war by entering battle himself. His miracles began the process of victory. They were battles against the powers of darkness that had fallen on God's people. Jesus himself explained his ministry as a military campaign: "He has sent me to proclaim freedom for the prisoners and recovery of sight for the blind, to release the oppressed" (Luke 4:18).

Christ moved more decisively against evil in his death and resurrection. We do not usually think of these great events as battles, but that is precisely what they were. Christ's substitutionary death canceled the curse of sin and destroyed the power of evil forces that had once enslaved us. As Paul put it, "And having disarmed the powers and authorities, he made a public spectacle of them, triumphing over them by the cross" (Col. 2:15).

Beyond this, Christ used his resurrection power to capture the forces of evil. Then from heaven he poured forth gifts of victory on the church: "But to each one of us grace has been given as Christ apportioned it. This is why it says: 'When he ascended on high, he led captives in his train and gave gifts to men.' . . . It was he who gave some to be apostles, some to be prophets, some to be evangelists, and some to be pastors and teachers" (Eph. 4:7–8, 11).

As the New Testament reveals, Christ defeated evil through the cross and distributed the joys of victory through his resurrection.

The spiritual side of Christ's battle continues today in the church. He is equipping the church to continue the fight that he began. This is why Paul exhorted the Ephesians to join in spiritual warfare:

> Finally, be strong in the Lord and in his mighty power. Put on the full armor of God so that you can take your stand against the devil's schemes. For our struggle is not against flesh and blood, but against the rulers, against the authorities, against the powers of this dark world and against the spiritual forces of evil in the heavenly realms. Therefore put on the full armor of God, so that when the day of evil comes, you may be able to stand your ground, and after you have done everything, to stand. (Eph. 6:10–13)

Believers throughout the world are engaged in a spiritual battle against the powers of darkness. The Evil One and his angels constantly seek to destroy us. What are we to do? Twice the apostle says, "Put on the full armor of God" (vv. 11, 13). What are the parts of this armor? The list is familiar: the belt of truth, the breastplate of righteousness, the shoes of the preparation of the gospel, the shield of faith, the helmet of salvation, and the sword of the Spirit (vv. 14–17). In addition to this armor, Paul encouraged the Ephesians to "pray in the Spirit on all occasions with all kinds of prayers and requests" (v. 18).

If we follow Paul's counsel, success in our spiritual warfare is assured. As he put it, "When the day of evil comes, you may be able to stand your ground, and after you have done everything, to stand" (v. 13). Christ's warfare continues today as you and I battle in his armor and power. In this way, we see the spiritual side of God's promises for ancient Israel fulfilled in our lives.

The victories already won by Christ are grand, but they hardly compare with the last battle that will occur at his second coming. Christ will destroy "the man of lawlessness" (2 Thess. 2:3) and send Satan and his host to everlasting fire (Rev. 20:10).

At that time, Christ's holy war will be completed by a cataclysmic victory. The apostle John describes the glorious end of Christ's holy war:

> I saw heaven standing open and there before me was a white horse, whose rider is called Faithful and True. With justice he judges and makes war. His eyes are like blazing fire, and on his head are many crowns. He has a name written on him that no one knows but he himself. He is dressed in a robe dipped in blood, and his name is the Word of God. The armies of heaven were following him, riding on white horses and dressed in fine linen, white and clean. Out of his mouth comes a sharp sword with which to strike down the nations. "He will rule them with an iron scepter." He treads the winepress of the fury of the wrath of God Almighty. On his robe and on his thigh he has this name written: KING OF KINGS AND LORD OF LORDS. (Rev. 19:11–16)

What will be the outcome of this final battle? The armies of earth will be "killed with the sword that came out of the mouth of the rider on the horse, and all the birds [will gorge] themselves on their flesh" (Rev. 19:21). Then the people of God will rise up and receive the spoils of Christ's victory as an eternal possession.

Moses prepared Israel for holy war because dignity for God's redeemed images would come through struggle and victory over evil. Old Testament Israel experienced only temporary victories and eventually suffered terrible defeat because of her sin. But we should not give up hope. We now see that the war belongs to Christ. He is the conqueror, the one who defeats evil and grants victory to his people. Christ is the last step in the restoration of God's image.

CHRIST AND DAVID

"Four More Years! Four More Years! Four More Years!" So the crowds shout as hopes build that an American president will win a second term. Significant success in a president's first term nearly insures reelection. Everyone expects more good things in the future. "We've been able to do a lot," the candidates assure their applauding supporters, "but the future holds even greater things for our country."

In chapter 7 we looked at David's celebration of his political success. God poured a special measure of his grace on Israel in the days of David to lift his people to greater heights of dignity. He transformed the nation from a loose confederation of tribes into a strong nation. David, as well as many of his sons, accomplished much as they ruled over Israel.

Nevertheless, the Old Testament records a sad end for the house of David. The sin of David's sons caused God to remove the throne from Jerusalem. The nation and her king went into exile in Babylon. The prophets foretold that a descendant of David would restore the nation. Hopes were stirred when Zerubbabel led some Judahites back to the land and rebuilt the temple. But the desire for a new, righteous David to sit on the throne in Jerusalem never materialized.

As we see the disarray of Israel's kingdom today, we have to wonder what happened to God's promises. Did he not assure David of an unending dynasty? Whatever became of the kingdom blessings promised to Israel?

The New Testament answers these questions by identifying Jesus as the heir to David's throne. Matthew and Luke composed extensive genealogies to demonstrate that he was the descendant of David (Matt. 1:1–17; Luke 3:23–38). Jesus was born in Bethlehem, the city of David (Luke 2:4–7). As David's final heir, Jesus brings incomparable kingdom blessings to God's redeemed images. He fulfills all the hopes of honor associated with the royal line in ways that go far beyond what David and his other sons ever accomplished.

The blessings of Christ's kingdom encompass a vast array of benefits for the image of God. To gain a glimpse of what Christ does for us, we will focus on three blessings that came through the line of David during the Old Testament period. Then we will see how Christ brings these gifts to God's people in the New Testament age.

First, David's house was to provide protection for Israel against evil. David and his sons had the responsibility of safeguarding the nation. Even when the conquest of the land subsided, the royal house had the responsibility of providing security. For this reason, the kings of Israel erected city walls and maintained armies. Every responsible member of David's house devised ways to protect the people.

Second, the royal line of Judah was to insure prosperity for God's people. Within the walls of royal protection, Israel prospered beyond measure. Righteousness prevailed when the Law of Moses was enforced by the king. People could live and work without fear of criminals. Economic conditions improved as David's sons did their jobs properly. When kings ruled over the land in righteousness, the people prospered. The house of David not only protected God's people from their enemies but also brought prosperity to the land.

Third, David's house was divinely ordained to insure the special presence of God among the people. David spent his life preparing for the temple, a permanent edifice for the presence of God. Solomon constructed the temple at the center of his kingdom. The kings of Judah always bore the responsibility of maintaining the proper functioning of the temple. Without the presence of God, all the efforts of the royal family were in vain. There could be no protection or prosperity without the presence of God. He responded to the prayers, sacrifices, and songs associated with the temple by pouring out his kingdom benefits on the people.

The kingdom blessings of protection, prosperity, and divine presence did not cease with the Old Testament. These ancient realities anticipated greater benefits to come in Christ. But we must remember that Jesus bestows these kingdom blessings in two stages. He brings protection, prosperity, and divine presence both in his first coming and in his return.

In his resurrection and ascension, Jesus rose to the throne of David and began to reign over the earth. As Peter told the Jews on the Day of Pentecost:

> Brothers, I can tell you confidently that the patriarch David died and was buried, and his tomb is here to this day. But he was a prophet and knew that God had promised him on oath that he would place one of his descendants on his throne. Seeing what was ahead, he spoke of the resurrection of the Christ, that he was not abandoned to the grave, nor did his body see decay. God has raised this Jesus to life, and we are all witnesses of the fact. (Acts 2:29–32)

From his exalted position, Jesus bestowed kingdom benefits on the people of God.

At this initial stage, Christ's blessings were primarily spiritual in nature. Jesus guaranteed his followers protection: "No one can snatch them out of my hand" (John 10:28). As 1 John 4:4 says, "The one who is in you is greater than the one who is in the world." Neither human nor supernatural forces can rob us of our salvation in Christ. As our king, Jesus protects each one of us.

Christ also blesses his people with spiritual prosperity. Paul said that we now possess "every spiritual blessing in Christ" (Eph. 1:3). Jesus said that he came "that they may have life, and have it to the full" (John 10:10). Christ guarantees spiritual prosperity to the people in his kingdom.

Finally, Christ provides the presence of God among his people. When Jesus left for heaven, he removed his physical presence. But he sent the Spirit to comfort his followers with the assurance of God's nearness. "I will not leave you as orphans; I will come to you" (John 14:18). For this reason, he could promise his apostles, "I am with you always, to the very end of the age" (Matt. 28:20).

The kingdom blessings that we enjoy today are grand, but we must remember that they are primarily spiritual. Christ does not promise us protection from all physical evil in this stage of his kingdom. In fact, he warned that his followers would suffer and be persecuted: "If they persecuted me, they will persecute you also" (John 15:20). Moreover, Christ's kingship does not guarantee material prosperity and health today. The trials of poverty and illness remain with many of us. Paul knew how to be "content . . . whether living in plenty or in want" (Phil. 4:12). Finally, Christ does not give us his physical presence at this time, either. He is present in the Spirit, but we long to see him and touch him again. The church now cries out, "Come, Lord Jesus" (Rev. 22:20).

While Christ only guarantees us spiritual blessings today, his protection, prosperity, and presence will extend even to physical levels when he returns. In the new creation we will be protected against all forms of evil, both physical and spiritual. The enemies of God will be utterly destroyed and we will have nothing to fear. "Then the end will come, when he hands over the kingdom to God the Father after he has destroyed all dominion, authority and power. For he must reign until he has put all his enemies under his feet. The last enemy to be destroyed is death" (1 Cor. 15:24–26).

In the fullness of Christ's kingdom, we will receive glorified physical bodies: "There are also heavenly bodies and there are earthly bodies; but the splendor of the heavenly bodies is one kind, and the splendor of the earthly bodies is another. . . . So will it be with the resurrection of the dead" (1 Cor. 15:40, 42).

All illness and grief will be gone. "There will be no more death or mourning or crying or pain" (Rev. 21:4). Finally, when Christ returns, we will no longer yearn to be in his physical presence—because he will be among us. We will know Christ's presence, both spiritually and physically. In his vision of the New Jerusalem, John "did not see a temple in the city, because the Lord God Almighty and the Lamb are its temple" (Rev. 21:22).

Christ fulfills all the hopes of the Davidic family. He brings the blessings of God's kingdom to all those who serve him faithfully. David and his sons brought outpourings of tremendous benefits for God's people, but those Old Testament blessings fell short of the dignity for which we were designed. Christ alone brings full kingdom blessings. He is the last step in the restoration of God's image.

CONCLUSION

In this chapter we have seen that the first and second coming of Christ form the last and most important step in our restoration. As the last Adam, Christ reversed the effects of Adam's sin. Like Noah, he brought judgment and a new world. He inherited and distributed the promises given to Abraham. As Moses prepared Israel for war, Jesus won the victory for God's people. Like David, Christ brought the blessings of God's kingdom to us. The full restoration of God's image finally depends on the efforts of

the one person in whom we must place all of our hopes—
Jesus Christ. *He* is the last step toward dignity.

ẽ&   ẽ&   ẽ&

REVIEW QUESTIONS

1. Why does the New Testament speak of Christ as the
   "last Adam"? How is Adam's sin reversed by Christ?
2. Explain how Christ is like Noah in his first coming and
   in his return.
3. How does the New Testament connect Jesus to Abraham? What are the implications of this connection?
4. How does Christ complete the holy war begun by Moses
   and Joshua?
5. What kingdom blessings does Christ bring as the son of
   David?

DISCUSSION EXERCISES

1. Why is this chapter entitled "Taking the Last Step"?
2. List five reasons why you and I cannot put our confidence in Adam, Noah, Abraham, Moses, and David.
   Why do we have to look to Christ for restoration?
3. Make four positive and negative comparisons of Christ
   with Noah, Abraham, Moses, and David. How do these
   comparisons draw you toward Christ as the only hope
   for restoration?
4. Identify five ways in which Christ's first coming did not
   complete our restoration to dignity. How will these be
   resolved when he returns?

10

HOLDING ON UNTIL
WE GET THERE

It happens on nearly every family vacation and it drives parents crazy. "Are we there yet?" the children ask from the back seat. "How much longer? . . . How much farther now?"

"Fifty feet less than the last time you asked!" the frustrated father shouts.

Then Mom intervenes to keep the peace. "This trip is going to take some time, kids. . . . You'll have to hold on 'til we get there," she advises.

Long trips are hard for children. They feel trapped in the back seat, but we know that the journey will not last too long. So we encourage them to hold on until they get there.

This book has taken us on a long journey. We have seen what God made the human race in the beginning, what we have made of ourselves throughout history, and what God has made it possible for us to be through his gracious gifts in the days of Noah, Abraham, Moses, David, and Christ. We have come a long way down the road to dignity, but a lot of traveling still lies before us. While God has already accomplished much for humanity, each of us must deal with the struggle of living prior to Christ's return. At times, we look at our lives and wonder, "How much farther? . . . How much longer?" How can we endure having come so far, but not far enough? How can we hold on until we get there?

In this chapter we will look for insight into the last leg of our journey by examining Romans 8:17–39. This passage describes two realities that lie ahead of us in the Christian life. On the one hand, we learn that our path is fraught with suffering. As wonderful as it is to follow Christ, the way to dignity is still a way of hardship. On the other hand, we also find that there is help for those who grow weary in their trials. God has provided encouragement to keep us moving ahead. If we hope to complete our journey to dignity, we must embrace both sides of the Christian life. We must reckon with the suffering to which we have been called and lay hold of the encouragement that God has made available to us (see Figure 10).

Figure 10. Suffering and Encouragement Ahead of Us

OUR CALL TO SUFFERING

I love to write. No, that's not true. I love to have written. When I see one of my books on the shelf, I have a sense of accomplishment—but the process of writing nearly kills me. Some of my colleagues can write as easily as they speak, but not me. Every page is a painful ordeal. Editing and reediting, again and again—it's never easy. Why do I put up with all this grief? The answer is simple. I cannot finish a book unless I go through the suffering that it requires. I can't enjoy one without enduring the other.

In the latter half of the eighth chapter of Romans, Paul describes the Christian life in a similar way. He introduces the theme of suffering as he sums up the blessings that God's children receive: "Now if we are children, then we are heirs—heirs of God and coheirs with Christ, if indeed we share in his sufferings in order that we may also share in his glory" (Rom. 8:17).

As God's children, we confidently expect to receive a grand inheritance from our heavenly Father. We are coheirs with Christ, sharing in the dignity of his wondrous riches. But as Paul indicates in this passage, we are not simply joint heirs in Christ's honor. We are also coheirs of his suffering; we suffer as Christ suffered.

Paul has thrown us a curve ball, hasn't he? Throughout this book we have focused on dignity, not suffering. We have seen God's plan to move his people away from ignobility and toward full restoration as his glorious images. But now Paul tells us that Christians inherit the suffering of Jesus. What has suffering to do with God's plan to restore us to dignity? How does it fit in?

As mysterious as it may seem, God has ordained suffering as the path to dignity. Enduring hardship is the means by which we receive glory. Notice again how plainly Paul puts it: "We share in his sufferings *in order that* we may also share in his glory" (Rom. 8:17, emphasis added). We simply cannot enjoy Christ's glory without participating in his suffering.

To understand the place of hardship in the Christian life, we must be clear about what kind of suffering Paul has in mind. Troubles come upon believers for many reasons. We can distinguish at least three kinds of suffering.

First, our lives are riddled with difficulties simply because we live in a fallen world. God has not entirely lifted the curse he placed on creation when Adam and Eve sinned (Gen. 3:16–19). Even Christ did not completely deliver us from the troubles our first parents brought upon us. Believers endure many hardships common to the human race. We are victims of injustice; we endure the ravages of war; we suffer natural disasters; we become ill and die. These kinds of difficulties do not occur because we have personally disobeyed God. Rather, we go through them because we live in a world cursed by Adam's sin.

Second, believers suffer as a direct result of their personal unrighteousness. Violations of God's moral standards bring many miseries into our lives. Adultery leads to divorce; stealing leads to imprisonment. We suffer these kinds of troubles because they are consequences of our disobedience. More than this, our sins often stir up God's chastisement against us. He disciplines his wandering children with difficulties in order to bring them back to the path of righteousness (Heb. 12:10). In both of these ways, our personal sins cause us to suffer.

These troubles make life difficult enough, but Paul does not have them in mind when he says, "We share in [Christ's] sufferings" (Rom. 8:17). He is concerned with a third type of suffering—troubles that God has specifically ordained for followers of Christ. We experience hardships because God has called us to suffer.

Every Christian has been called to suffering in at least two ways. On the one hand, we share the sufferings of Christ because our devotion to him angers the world. The words of Jesus are to the point: "If the world hates you, keep in mind that it hated me first" (John 15:18). We stand with the One whom the world of darkness hates. Consequently, unbelievers persecute us as they persecuted him.

History records how countless Christians have endured terrible trials at the hands of unbelievers. Even today believers suffer horrendous persecution in some parts of the world. The influence of the gospel on the nations keeps many of us from suffering severely, but the world's hatred for God's redeemed images still manifests itself. Professional organizations reject us. Neighbors and family members exclude us. In these and many other ways, we suffer for Christ because the world sets itself against us.

Paul warned Timothy that "everyone who wants to live a godly life in Christ Jesus will be persecuted" (2 Tim. 3:12). These words should stir us to serious self-reflection. If you and I do not experience some kind of trouble from the world, we should wonder about the strength of our commitment to Christ. Those who follow the call of Jesus set themselves on a collision course with unbelievers. Conflict and persecution are inevitable.

On the other hand, Christians also suffer because God has called us to deny our own desires and adopt a life of sacrificial service. This aspect of Christian experience becomes evident in several New Testament passages. In 2 Corinthians 1:5, Paul wrote that "the sufferings of Christ flow over into our lives." Humiliation and service were not just for Jesus—his sufferings spill over into the experience of the church. In much the same way, Paul spoke of his ministry as the opportunity to "fill up in my flesh what is still lacking in regard to Christ's afflictions, for the sake of his body, which is the church" (Col. 1:24). We continue in Christ's sufferings by following his footsteps of sacrificial service.

When men and women place their faith in Christ, God supernaturally joins them to Christ's death and resurrection (Rom. 6:1–7). In effect, what happened to him two thousand years ago happens to us; we "died to sin" (v. 2) and are resurrected to "new life" (v. 4). Yet, as we live on this side of glory, our union with Christ also entails continuing his earthly humiliation. Christ "did not come to be served, but to serve" (Mark 10:45). He "was rich, yet for your sakes he became poor" (2 Cor. 8:9). He forsook his own honor "to seek and to save what was lost" (Luke 19:10). He "humbled himself and became obedient to death—even death on a cross!" (Phil. 2:8). To live for Christ is to live as he lived. We do not seek to be served, but to serve; we do not strive to gain the treasures of this life, but to lose them for him.

In this light, it should be evident that God has not simply called us to *endure* suffering for Christ's sake. He expects us to *volunteer* for suffering. How did Jesus put it? "If anyone would come after me, he must deny himself and take up his cross daily and follow me" (Luke 9:23). To follow Christ is to volunteer for trouble. Paul expressed the desire that should be in all of our hearts when he said, "I want to know Christ and the power of his resurrection and the fellowship of sharing in his sufferings" (Phil. 3:10). Believers should not suffer for Christ begrudgingly; we should long to share in his trials.

All honorable soldiers deserve our respect. They face threatening circumstances and often sacrifice their lives for others. We should acknowledge the courage of every soldier, but our hearts swell with a special appreciation for those who volunteer for war. They freely put aside the goals of their lives and deny themselves home and loved ones in order to live and perhaps die for others.

Let's face it. More often than not, we are draftees of suffering, not volunteers. When events beyond our control force us to sacrifice, we bear up under the load as best we can. But we seldom purposefully deny our own desires in order to take up the cross of Christ. We are too interested in comfort to volunteer for suffering. As coheirs of Christ's sufferings, however, we must set aside our personal goals for the sake of the kingdom. Of course, we must be wise stewards of the possessions and successes God gives us in this world. But men and women who set their hearts on hoarding possessions and wielding earthly power fail to live as those joined to Christ. God has called us to look for ways to share in Christ's suffering.

I have a friend who knows how to deny himself for Christ. He left his upper middle-class home and moved into

[handwritten margin note: we should volunteer pg 185]

the inner city to minister to teens. He quickly made friends with several young men and invited them to his apartment for a Bible study. After they spent an hour or so in the Scriptures, my friend went down the block to buy some refreshments. He returned twenty minutes later to find that his new acquaintances had robbed him of his television, stereo, and bicycle.

"How did it make you feel?" I asked him.

"I was angry at first," he confessed, "but then it hit me. If Jesus sacrificed so much for me, then I can sacrifice these little things for him."

How does God want you and me to suffer? Every person must decide individually before the Lord. God calls some Christians to radical sacrifice: foreign missions, service to the poor, and a host of similar vocations require tremendous self-denial. God calls other Christians to volunteer for suffering in other ways. We can give generously to Christian ministries, instead of keeping every spare penny for ourselves. We can donate time to evangelism and service, instead of filling our lives with our own projects. We can make career decisions that honor Christ, instead of those that honor us. We can work hard on a failing marriage, instead of seeking a divorce. We can open our homes to those in need, instead of buying a new car. We can visit the elderly and the sick, instead of staring at the television. The opportunities are endless if we will only look for them.

Unfortunately, many Christian groups have taken their eyes off our call to suffering. In some circles, the necessity of suffering is displaced by an emphasis on material prosperity. Listen to Christian radio and television. You'll hear plenty of preachers tell their listeners that they do not need to endure hardships. "The Lord wants you to prosper," they insist. "Believe that you will get that new car and that big house!" To be sure, there is nothing wrong with prosperity in itself. "The love of money"—not the possession of money—"is a root of all kinds of evil" (1 Tim. 6:10). In fact, wealthy Christians have tremendous opportunities to use their resources for Christ. Nonetheless, an overemphasis on material prosperity often causes us to neglect asking how God wants us to deny ourselves for Christ.

Whenever material prosperity becomes our dominant concern, we should remember Jesus' poverty. As he said, "Foxes have holes and birds of the air have nests, but the Son of Man has no place to lay his head" (Luke 9:58). Christ did not lack faith. He was not out of accord with God's will. He simply knew that God had called him to sacrificial service. Christ's trust in the Father actually caused him to deny himself the riches of this world for the glory of the next world. As men and women joined to Christ, we should be ready to suffer in the same way.

In some circles, believers' eyes are drawn away from voluntary self-denial by a focus on gaining power and influence in the world. "Christians must become leaders and establish Christian principles," they cry. "To do this we must have power!"

This view contains an important element of truth. Christ called his followers to be the salt and light of the world (Matt. 5:13–16). We are to fulfill the cultural mandate by taking the lead in every aspect of culture. But a serious danger lurks behind an overemphasis on this side of our lives. Our hopes and dreams easily become so attached to success here that we cannot see the ways in which we must sacrifice. "Climb the corporate ladder! Work your way to the top!" we urge. Don't misunderstand me. With the proper motivations, rising to leadership in any field can be an act of self-denial. Good leaders do not live for themselves; they are hardworking servants. But we must be careful not to focus so much on gaining power that we forget the importance of self-denial in this life.

The kingdom of Christ has made great strides toward influencing the world, and it will continue to do so in the future. We can be sure that "the gates of Hades will not overcome it" (Matt. 16:18). Even so, history teaches us that Christ's kingdom influences the world more when we stop grabbing for earthly power and embrace the suffering to which we have been called. It is in our weakness that Christ's strength is manifested (2 Cor. 12:9).

We should expect suffering as we travel the road to dignity. Believers endure common troubles in the world and bear the consequences of sin. But more than this, God calls us to suffer voluntarily by enduring persecution and sacrificing our own desires for him. With all these ways of suffering before us, we have to ask an honest question. How can we continue down the road to dignity with this much hardship? Paul addresses this question in the remainder of the eighth chapter of Romans.

ENCOURAGEMENT FROM THE FUTURE

Anyone who stays in the hospital for a long time will tell you that the experience can be overwhelming. Discouragement quickly moves to depression as you lie in bed week after week. I remember once speaking with a cancer patient who kept an extraordinarily positive attitude through a long stay in the hospital. "How do you do it?" I asked him.

"I know I'm going to get better," he explained, "I get a perspective on what's happening now by keeping my eyes on the future."

We have seen that Christians should expect, even volunteer, for suffering in this life. Sometimes, however, these difficulties get the best of us. Like patients in a hospital, we can feel overwhelmed by our troubles. What should we do when these anxieties rise within us? We must get a perspective on our sufferings by keeping our eyes on the future.

Paul confidently asserts that our current hardships cannot compare with the wonder of our future. He put the matter succinctly: "I consider that our present sufferings are not worth comparing with the glory that will be revealed in us" (Rom. 8:18). Although the Christian life entails suffering, the brilliance of our final destiny drives away the shadows of trials. When compared to our future glory, our present difficulties seem like nothing.

These words did not come from the pen of an armchair theologian. They were not merely theory for Paul. He spoke as one whose life was filled with self-denial for Christ. Few saints have endured as many hardships as he. He left his homeland, traveled across treacherous seas, and preached to angry crowds. He was falsely accused, beaten, and imprisoned. He volunteered for these and countless other trials for the sake of Christ. Yet, Paul knew how to keep his sufferings in perspective. They did not overwhelm him because he looked forward to the second coming of Christ. Recognizing the glory of the consummation made the difficulties of his life seem insignificant. They were "not worth comparing" (Rom. 8:18).

A fellow minister came to me one day with a heavy burden. His ministry was in a mess. A group of disgruntled members had left his church and he was deeply discouraged. "I don't think I can stand it," he said. "I give all I have and get no reward. It's just not worth it."

This minister was closer to the truth than he realized. The sacrifices he made as a servant of the church were not worth the rewards he received in this life. He experienced a few high points here and there. His small successes brought moments of relief from his struggles, but every new day led him into situations that demanded more self-denial. So long as he focused his heart on the rewards of this world, he would have to conclude that the pain was not worth it.

From time to time, all of us face this kind of discouragement. We devote ourselves to parenting. We work hard to live as Christian businesspeople. We sacrifice time and energy to one ministry after another. But what do we have to show for years of service? Only demands for more sacrifice. "If this is all that comes from my suffering, I just can't continue," we lament.

The cost of sacrificial service to Christ is not worth the results we see in this life. We receive blessings that encourage us along the way: business successes, faithful children, and good health. But these gifts alone cannot sustain those whose lives are filled with voluntary suffering. They are but sips of water along the Via Dolorosa. To overcome the discouragement that often accompanies suffering, we must follow Paul's example by turning away from this life and focusing on our reward in the world to come.

Our problems are complicated by another matter. Even when we think about the wonder of Christ's return, we seldom consider much more than our own personal salvation. Personal redemption is a wonderful gift from God. We look forward to eternal life without sadness, guilt, and disappointments. But our vision needs to be enlarged if we hope to gain encouragement from the future.

As Paul reflected on the return of Christ, he focused on more than his personal salvation. He looked ahead to the astounding cosmic redemption that will take place:

The creation waits in eager expectation for the sons of God to be revealed. For the creation was subjected to frustration, not by its own choice, but by the will of the one who subjected it, in hope that the creation itself will be liberated from its bondage to decay and brought into the glorious freedom of the children of God. We know that the whole creation has been groaning as in the pains of childbirth right up to the present time. (Rom. 8:19–22)

Something much more spectacular than the salvation of our souls is waiting at the end of the road to dignity. Our full restoration will be accompanied by a renewal of the whole creation. The universe fell under God's curse when Adam and Eve sinned. The wondrous creation was subjected to futility and decay, but not without hope for a brighter future. When Christ returns and rescues us from the curse of death, he will also dramatically renew everything else in God's creation: the mountains and valleys, the deserts and seas, the plants and animals. Our solar system, the galaxy, and even the entire universe will be restored to their original splendor. Harmony will replace discord. Beauty will replace decay and destruction. Then comes the most astounding part of it all. All of this new creation, every square inch of it, will be placed beneath our feet forever. "The meek," Jesus said, "will inherit the earth" (Matt. 5:5).

Paul occupied his heart with thoughts of the grand redemption to come in Christ. When hardships approached, he bathed himself in the glory of reigning in a new creation set free from futility. He looked with unspeakable delight at the joy that would be his. With this vision of the future he could look back on his suffering and know that it was all worth it.

A former student of mine passed away recently. About two years ago, the doctors gave him only a few months to live. He suffered from fatigue and pain, but he kept ministering to the very end. He and his wife came to visit one day and I had the opportunity to ask him some hard questions. "How do you keep going when you know you're going to die soon?" I queried. I will never forget his answer.

"Look, Richard," he said with a smile, "going home to Jesus is more real to me than it has ever been. I'm making it now because I see better than ever how good it will be when I go home."

Those words have come back to me many times. They give me strength when I grow weary. You can make them a part of your life, too. When troubles get you down, look ahead and see how good it will be when you go home to the new heavens and the new earth. The glory of the future is God's encouragement for all who suffer now.

ENCOURAGEMENT FROM THE SPIRIT

We have all heard reports of the horrors faced by prisoners of war. Torture, deprivation, and disease take their toll on captured soldiers. But one cruelty stands out in many accounts: the prison within a prison—solitary confinement. Separated from all contact with others, a POW has no means of support or encouragement. By comparison, the prison block is a world of freedom where prisoners strengthen and help each other. But in solitary confinement, the POW is utterly abandoned, left to face his captivity alone.

As we have seen, Christians have been confined to a time of suffering before they receive the glory of Christ. We look forward to a day of release, but that day often seems far away. We need something here and now to lighten our burden. What encouragement can we find in this life? Is there someone to share our burdens, or do we have to suffer in the loneliness of solitary confinement?

In Romans 8:22–27, Paul continues his words of encouragement by directing our attention to the support we can find in the midst of our trials. He affirms that following Christ can be very difficult at times, but he reminds us that we do not face this time of trouble in isolation. God has sent his Spirit to help us bear the cross of suffering:

> We know that the whole creation has been groaning as in the pains of childbirth right up to the present time. Not only so, but we ourselves, who have the firstfruits of the Spirit, groan inwardly as we wait eagerly for our adoption as sons, the redemption of our bodies. For in this hope we were saved. But hope that is seen is no hope at all. Who hopes for what he already has? But if we hope for what we do not yet have, we wait for it patiently. In the same way, the Spirit helps us in our weakness. We do not know what we ought to pray for, but the Spirit himself intercedes for us with groans that words cannot express. And he who searches our hearts knows the mind of the Spirit, because the Spirit intercedes for the saints in accordance with God's will. (Rom. 8:22–27)

Paul begins this passage with a remarkable admission. He honestly acknowledges that Christians often "groan inwardly" (v. 23) under the pressures of suffering. Our lot becomes so difficult at times that "we do not know what we ought to pray for" (v. 26).

But we are not left alone in this condition. We have "the firstfruits of the Spirit" (v. 23), who "helps us in our weakness" (v. 26). The Spirit does many things to minister to us, but Paul focuses on a particular aspect of his work. When we groan under the weight of waiting for our glory to be revealed, the Spirit "intercedes for us with groans that words cannot express" (v. 26). The Holy Spirit feels our pain and bears our burdens before the Father. These are no ordinary prayers: "And he who searches our hearts knows the mind of the Spirit, because the Spirit intercedes for the saints in accordance with God's will" (v. 27).

Our heavenly Father listens to the Spirit because he intercedes in a way that always pleases the Father. When we are discouraged and forlorn to the point that we are speechless, the Spirit cares and speaks for us.

At first glance, we have to wonder what relevance Paul's words have for those who suffer. After all, the intercessory groaning of the Spirit is imperceptible. We cannot hear him sharing our burdens, nor can we observe his pleas to the Father. How can an abstract teaching like this offer us practical encouragement? What comfort can we derive from a ministry of the Spirit that we cannot perceive?

In an important sense, simply knowing this theological truth affords some measure of encouragement. It is good to understand that the Spirit is with us in our suffering. As is the case with many doctrines of Scripture, accepting this invisible reality helps us properly understand the visible world in which we live. When we learn that the Spirit of God groans with us, we can take heart. When we believe that he prays perfectly for us, we can gain strength. Even as abstract truths, these beliefs offer some help to those who suffer.

At the same time, however, reducing the work of the Spirit to an abstraction makes it difficult for us to feel the reassurance Paul offers in this passage. To grasp the full import of his words, we must remember something about the Roman Christians to whom he wrote.

Paul conveyed much more than theoretical truth to his original readers. The believers in Rome knew the reality of the Spirit's presence in ways that go far beyond what most believers experience today. Their lives were filled with perceptible manifestations of the Spirit everywhere they turned. Consider the list of gifts existing in the Roman church: prophesying, serving, teaching, encouraging, giving, leadership, and mercy (Rom. 12:3–8). The Spirit was no stranger to Paul's readers. Every day they saw astounding demonstrations of his power and love. His presence was not something they accepted in spite of their experience. Rather, they knew him because of their experience. Paul's words about the imperceptible ministry of the Spirit lifted the hearts of the Roman church because they saw evidence of the Spirit's presence day after day.

When my wife and I were students, we earned extra money by house-sitting and taking care of children while their parents traveled. On one occasion, a little boy fell down and badly bruised his knee. I tried to comfort him, but it was no use. He cried and cried for his mother. After an hour or so, we decided to call the boy's mom long distance. When the little boy heard his mother's voice, he immediately began to calm down. Even though she was far away, his pain subsided because he knew that his mother was sharing his hurt.

Why did that phone call make such a difference? That child was used to being with his mother. He had experienced her tender touch and soothing presence many times over the years. With those memories in his heart, he took comfort in her sympathy, even though she was far away.

The Roman Christians were in a similar position when Paul told them about the intercessions of the Holy Spirit.

Because these believers had experienced so many blessings of the Spirit, knowing about his distant work meant a great deal to them. They knew how wonderful he was, so they found tremendous encouragement in his sympathy and prayers.

Sadly, many Christians today find it difficult to receive much encouragement from the Holy Spirit because he is not very real to them. We seldom acknowledge the Spirit's power and love. Our churches are dull and ordinary; our lives are plain and commonplace. In a word, the Holy Spirit is a stranger to many of us. What good is the distant sympathy of a stranger? What comfort can we take in the prayers of someone we don't even know? Not much.

Is the Spirit gone from the church? Is he a stranger because he no longer ministers to us? Nothing could be further from the truth. If the Holy Spirit seems absent, it is only because we fail to appreciate the visible blessings he gives.

When it comes to perceiving that the Spirit is at work today, many believers remind me of an old "Three Stooges" gag. Curly screams at the top of his voice, "I can't see! I can't see! I can't see!" "What's wrong? What's wrong?" Moe responds. "I've got my eyes closed," Curly answers to the delight of the audience.

That's the way it is in the church today. We complain, "I can't see the Spirit at work! I can't see him! I can't see him!" But the problem is not that he has vanished. We can't see him because we have closed our eyes.

To receive encouragement from the Spirit's imperceptible sympathy and prayers, we must open our eyes and take full notice of the countless gifts he has lavished on us. Insights into Scripture, conviction of sin, success in evangelism, joy in our salvation, physical healings, gifts and leadership in the church, comfort in sorrow, love and fellowship among believers—the list is endless. These realities of the Christian life are not natural occurrences. They are the visible manifestations of God's Spirit in our lives.

If we would stop denying the Holy Spirit and start acknowledging his wonders, he would no longer be a stranger, but a dear friend. Then Paul's words of comfort to the Romans would encourage us. We would be able to find encouragement in our Friend, knowing that he shares in our suffering and prays on our behalf.

ENCOURAGEMENT FROM GOD'S PLAN

"Don't worry about it. I've got a plan," the man said to his wife as they sat in their broken-down car. They had spent several hours on the side of the road hoping that someone would come by. "I've got a plan that will fix everything," he assured her.

"Wait a minute. I want to hear what you're going to do," she objected. "I'm not so sure I can trust your plans anymore. It was your idea for us to take this deserted road to begin with."

That's the way it is with human schemes. They are often ill conceived and fail. When we're in trouble and others offer a way out, we have good reasons for being skeptical. Their ideas may actually get us into more trouble.

But God's plans are just the opposite. He never makes mistakes and he can accomplish all he has set out to do. We can be sure that his plans are wise and that they will succeed.

For this reason, Paul closes his encouragement to those who suffer for Christ by appealing to the plan of God. In Romans 8:28–39 he sketches the divine design that lies behind the suffering to which God has called us. What is God doing through our ordeals? What is his eternal purpose in our suffering as we continue down the road to dignity?

Paul begins his discussion of God's plan with a well-known verse: "And we know that in all things God works for the good of those who love him, who have been called according to his purpose" (Rom. 8:28). What a tremendous passage this is for those who suffer for Christ! It is no wonder that so many Christians cherish these words. God has a plan for our troubles; he will use them for our good.

Notice that this divine plan is all-encompassing. Every event—not just some or most—is for our good. The circumstances we face as suffering Christians can be terrible. The cost of following Christ can be great. We may lose friends, a job, a spouse, and even parents. We may suffer imprisonment and even death. But no matter how disappointing and discouraging our situations become, we know something that gives us hope. We know that God has a plan to turn our suffering into blessings.

Many people imagine that this passage is a general statement that applies to every person. "Everything eventually works out for everyone's benefit," they say. But this is not what Paul affirms. The promise of eventual goodness is only for those "who have been called according to his purpose" (Rom. 8:28). Good does not eventually come to those who remain apart from Christ. As sad as they are, present sufferings are but a foretaste of the eternal punishment facing men and women who are outside of Christ. Life can be a living hell for unbelievers; they endure many of the same trials as Christians. But the living hell of this world is nothing compared to actually living in the hell of eternity.

But when believers suffer for Christ, they are not getting a taste of their future. We are not on a road that leads to destruction, but on one that leads to dignity. The hardships along our way are means by which God brings us to glory.

Think of it this way. God calls us to troubles as surgeons invite us to their operating tables. Their knives inflict terrible pain. No sane person enjoys the ordeal of surgery. To deny the anguish is to lie. Nonetheless, we voluntarily submit to the knife. Why? We allow them to cut because the pain will bring about better health in the future.

Paul tells us here that the same thing is true of God. He tells us to submit to the knife of suffering for Christ for

194

the good it will bring to us. God is working all of our troubles into something wonderful for us. We can submit to his call because he promises to work the pain for our good.

This perspective on the plan of God causes us to breathe a sigh of relief. We can all remember times when we have seen God bring good out of bad. We lose friends because we take a stand for Christ, but we find new and better friends somewhere else. We lose a job because of our Christian testimony, but God gives us a better one. We have all gone through hard times and seen God bring dramatic benefits out of them.

Nonetheless, doubts still linger; something troubles us. Many times we face troubles with no positive results. We go through suffering and never see God use it for our good. Sometimes we wait a lifetime wondering why God called us to particular situations. "What happened to God's plan?" we wonder. "How firm is his commitment to his promise?"

Paul realized that Christians have to deal with these questions. So he leads us further into the mind of God to assure us that God is absolutely resolute in his commitment to bringing good out of our trials: "For those God foreknew he also predestined to be conformed to the likeness of his Son, that he might be the firstborn among many brothers. And those he predestined, he also called; those he called, he also justified; those he justified, he also glorified" (Rom. 8:29–30).

In this passage, Paul reaches into eternity past. Before the world came into being, God mapped out a design for those who are called to Christ. He fixed a detailed design by a sovereign, immutable decree. Paul mentions five things that God determined on our behalf in his eternal counsel. When we understand these aspects of God's plan, we can rest assured that he is fully determined to work all things for our good.

First, God "foreknew" us (v. 29). Notice that this passage does not say that God foreknew what we would do. He knew *us* in an intimate and personal way. Before the universe was created, God gave individual and personal attention to us. From the infinite recesses of eternity, God cared for you and me with tender love and affection.

Second, God "predestined" us (v. 29). The Creator took such special interest in you and me that he actually settled ahead of time the direction our lives would take. Our future is not subject to the winds of change. We cannot veer off course. We are sovereignly "predestined to be conformed to the likeness of his Son, that he might be the firstborn among many brothers" (v. 29). Through his resurrection, Christ became the glorious image of God, but God did not intend for Christ to be his only honored image. On the contrary, the Father determined to have Christ be the first of many brothers and sisters who would be made like him. Men and women in Christ had their futures absolutely determined before the world even existed. They were designed for the dignity of conformity to Christ.

Third, God "called" us to himself (v. 30). He did not merely set us on a predetermined course toward dignity. He also ordained the means by which we would follow that course in history. God resolved to have us hear and respond to the call of the gospel. Your conversion was not the result of happenstance or good luck. It was no historical accident that you received the gospel. God eternally determined that the Spirit would move in your heart and bring you to repentance and saving faith.

Fourth, God "justified" us (v. 30). *Justify* is a legal term meaning "declare righteous." God rendered a legal verdict on our behalf. Instead of holding us responsible for our sins, he transferred our guilt to Christ and declared us freely forgiven. Had God left us to find our own way to righteousness, we would never be restored to dignity. But God was so determined that we should receive the blessing of full restoration that he punished his own Son in our place and transferred his righteousness to us.

Fifth, God "glorified" us (v. 30). Did you notice the tense of this verb? Paul does not say that God "will glorify" us. That is true enough; we will be glorified when Christ returns. But Paul is still thinking about God's plan in eternity past. From God's eternal perspective, we have already been glorified. Our full redemption is not something that hangs in the balance of future events. It is as good as done.

Now we can see how we can be confident that "in all things God works for the good of those who love him" (Rom. 8:28). God's plan is not open-ended. It is not something yet to be determined. Nothing has been left to chance. In his eternal counsel, God firmly anchored every step of history in order to bring us to our ultimate destiny in Christ.

When we grasp how God's unchanging eternal decrees secure our future, we can hold on to hope, even when the way to dignity becomes difficult. God will not immediately turn every event of suffering into a blessing, but eventually everything that happens, without exception, will be for our good.

Paul concludes his appeal to the plan of God with resounding confidence and praise. His words speak to the heart of every man and woman trying to hold on through the difficulties of life:

> What, then, shall we say in response to this? If God is for us, who can be against us? He who did not spare his own Son, but gave him up for us all—how will he not also, along with him, graciously give us all things? Who will bring any charge against those whom God has chosen? It is God who justifies. Who is he that condemns? Christ Jesus, who died—more than that, who was raised to life—is at the right hand of God and is also interceding for us. Who shall separate us from the love of Christ? Shall trouble or hardship or persecution or famine or nakedness or danger or sword? As it is written: "For your sake we face death all day long; we are considered as sheep to be slaughtered." No, in all these things we are more than conquerors through him who loved us.

> For I am convinced that neither death nor life, nei-
> ther angels nor demons, neither the present nor the
> future, nor any powers, neither height nor depth,
> nor anything else in all creation, will be able to sep-
> arate us from the love of God that is in Christ Je-
> sus our Lord. (Rom. 8:31–39)

Because God's plan for his redeemed image is so certain, we can face the worst difficulties, the most terrifying
enemies, and the most devastating ordeals with confidence.
We do not merely survive our trials; "we are more than conquerors" (v. 37) because absolutely nothing "will be able to
separate us from the love of God that is in Christ Jesus our
Lord" (v. 39).

CONCLUSION

In this chapter we have looked at two sides of our lives
as we continue down the road to dignity. While we still wait
for Christ to return, we have been called to suffer for him.
Every believer endures pain and hardship for Christ. But
this is only one side of the picture. God has also given us
encouragement to aid us in our suffering. He opens our
eyes to our glorious future; he gives us his Spirit; he alerts
us to his perfect plan. When we keep these encouragements
before our eyes, we can endure the worst suffering—we can
hold on until we get there.

ка   ка   ка

REVIEW QUESTIONS

1. Why is this chapter entitled "Holding On Until We Get
   There"?

2. What kinds of suffering take place in the world? What troubles have been reserved especially for believers?

3. How does our future help in our present circumstances? Describe the grandeur of the glory of Christ's return.

4. How does the presence of the Spirit encourage us during trials? Why do modern believers have so much trouble finding the encouragement of the Spirit?

5. How does God's plan help us to endure suffering? What is the goal of God's plan? How can we be sure that he is determined to carry it out?

DISCUSSION EXERCISES

1. Make a list of ten hardships you face. Divide the list into the categories of suffering suggested in this chapter.

2. Choose an area of your life (home, work, family, etc.). How does the present state of this area compare to the way it will be when Christ returns?

3. Look around your group. What visible work of the Holy Spirit can you identify? How do these works of the Spirit give you encouragement?

4. Name six problems you face. How does God's eternal plan give you confidence that you are "more than conquerors" in these difficulties?

INDEX OF SCRIPTURE